Idiotism

IDIOTISM

Capitalism and the
Privatisation of Life

Neal Curtis

First published 2013 by Pluto Press
345 Archway Road, London N6 5AA

www.plutobooks.com

British Library Cataloguing in Publication Data
A catalogue record for this book is available from the British Library

ISBN   978 0 7453 3156 0   Hardback
ISBN   978 0 7453 3155 3   Paperback
ISBN   978 1 8496 4788 5   PDF eBook
ISBN   978 1 8496 4790 8   Kindle eBook
ISBN   978 1 8496 4789 2   EPUB eBook

Library of Congress Cataloging in Publication Data applied f

10   9   8   7   6   5   4   3   2   1

Designed and produced for Pluto Press by Chase Publishing Services Ltd
Typeset from disk by Stanford DTP Services, Northampton, England

Contents

1
Enclosing the World, or Idiotism

This book was conceived in the aftermath of the 'Great Financial Crisis' (Bellamy and Magdoff 2009) that first came to public attention in 2008, but continued to devastate lives as I began to write in February 2011. No doubt it will continue to do so for many years to come, even as those most responsible quickly return to their multi-million dollar bonuses euphemistically referred to as 'compensation'. The state of the economy at the time of the crisis can be highlighted in a couple of quite startling facts that John Lanchester sets out in the opening chapter of his book *Whoops!*. First of all, throughout the years known as the war on terror, or economically speaking the security bubble, global GDP rose from $36 trillion dollars in 2000 to $70 trillion in 2006, largely driven by profits in the financial sector (2010:xii). Secondly, at the time of the crisis in 2008, the largest company in the world with assets of £1.9 trillion was a bank, the Royal Bank of Scotland. This is significant because the UK's GDP in 2008 was only £1.7 trillion (22). By any standard these figures are extraordinary. However, considering that regulation of the financial sector was negligible there was little if any oversight of this anabolic growth. This was because, according to Robert Lucas, Chicago University professor and 1995 Nobel prize winner, 'the "central problem of depression-prevention [...] has been solved"' (in Krugman 2008:9). This supposedly overcame the need for state regulation or intervention in line with the old Keynesian model. The market alone – run by and for an oligarchy of plutocrats also known as the 'Super Rich' – was sufficient. Even more disturbing is that despite the crisis, and not withstanding some minor technical adjustments, nothing has really changed. Even if we exit this crisis that is still to be played out in the sovereign debt crises of the Euro-zone and the US, many economists believe that a second crash will not be far off.

The roots of the crisis stem from an ideology of privatisation and free markets that goes back a long way. The idea that the pursuit of private interests in a free market of goods and services is the best way to achieve the common good can be traced back to the eighteenth-century liberalism of Adam Smith, but the idea that common land is more productive under private ownership dates back to the seventeenth century and the work of William Petty and John Locke. Locke in particular gave the philosophical justification for the enclosure of common land and resources that, aside from war (or increasingly in conjunction with war), remains capitalism's primary means of accumulation. However, while this long-standing privileging of the private is integral to our current socio-economic condition the most proximate causes of the crisis are quite recent, stemming from the financialisation of the economy that began in the 1970s with the Thatcher government in the UK and the Reagan administration in the US. At that time conditions emerged for the ideology of free market economics to gain a much greater and more radical purchase on our political imagination. The media constantly relayed bulletins promoting competition, consumer choice, council house sales, upward mobility, credit, privatisation, deregulation, designer labels, branding, gentrification, and the democracy of share options. Everyone was encouraged to join in the fiction of this new wealth and the seemingly endless supply of money created by the great sell off. Even the UK's pop stars were dressing up like bankers. We all lived in the brave new world of the Square Mile. Likewise in the US, the counter-culture that a decade earlier had preached resistance and the importance of finding onseself were now seamlessly folded into the niche-marketing of lifestyle choices and the new individualism.

By 1997 the emergence of New Labour in the UK under the leadership of Tony Blair came to signal the completion of a consensus around financialisation and privatisation that had shifted from the terrain of ideology to increasingly become part of a new common sense. By this I mean to say something akin to the popular folklore that Antonio Gramsci (1971:419) attributes to this term: something that is shaped by a coherent ideology, in turn supported by 'the great systems of traditional philosophy' (420), in this case utilitarianism and positivism, but remains 'ambiguous, contradictory and multiform' (423), retaining elements of nationalism, and racism, for example, mixed in with the new language of supposedly neutral, free market universalism. Nevertheless, despite elements of incoherence this new common sense projected a dominant conception of the world, one in which socialism, certainly, but even the postwar Welfare State and the politics of the New Deal were seen to be out of date. In this respect the use of the financial crisis to make a renewed case against public spending was the key to getting rid of the anachronistic, yet stubborn element of welfarism that had continued to survive in a much reduced capacity within it. Although the New Labour government claimed to be pursuing a social democratic agenda and believed in a public sector of sorts, Blair had been converted to the 'truth' of market fundamentalism, and like the Democratic presidency of Bill Clinton in the United States did much to further entrench the power of private forces both nationally and globally. Tony Blair's zeal for all things private and the Labour Party's conversion to the truth of market forces can also be explained in part by Gramsci's understanding of common sense because, as he points out, with common sense being 'crudely neophobe and conservative', the ability to bring about 'the introduction of a new truth is a proof that the truth in question has exceptional evidence and capacity for expansion' (423).

During the 1980s and 1990s, then, there was a great deal of debate amongst academics and activists about the nature of this new truth that was rapidly dismantling socialised economies around the globe and the cultures not predicated on consumption that stubbornly stood in its way. At a time when diversity and plurality were seen as democratic ideals to be promoted, and social and cultural theory was dominated by the discourses of hybridity and flow, it became increasingly apparent that powerful Western nations such as the USA and the UK, together with transnational capitalist institutions such as the WTO, the World Bank, and the IMF were becoming increasingly less tolerant of any form of social life that resisted the dogma of the global free market. Despite the ascendancy of multiculturalism free market capitalism increasingly became the only model for social organisation. In effect you can have free market capitalism with any kind of topping, but the stipulation is that you must have free market capitalism. For some, like many of the evangelical Christian communities in the US, an anti-state commitment to privatisation is an integral component of their cultural expression, for many others, however, it was an aside, and as long as the system permitted differentiated cultural expression the shape of the economy was of only a minor concern. For theorists like Michael Hardt and Antonio Negri (2000) the acceptance and encouragement of a variety of cultures went hand in hand with the post-Fordist model of capitalist growth via niche production and marketing where each cultural difference comes with its own glossy magazine. Rather than standing for something that countered a centralised dogma the 'multi' of multiculturalism underpinned the global extension of the free market and was used to legitimate it.

On this point it can be noted that one reason why radical Islam is so intolerable for the West is not because, as is primarily claimed, it threatens to role back centuries of political liberalism, but because it is opposed to economic liberalism and posits a clear alternative to our current economic formation. I would go so far as to say that even if a form of Islam emerged that supported many of the political freedoms the West recognises today – what we understand to be tolerance has its roots in Islamic civilisation after all – the West would remain as vehemently opposed to it precisely because of its challenge to current forms of socio-economic power. For example, while Christians (via Clavin) have conveniently found a way to forget the injunction against usury, it remains a pillar of Islamic economics. Thus, while the world has been increasingly opened up by travel, migration, cultural exchange and new technologies creating a heightened sense of global complexity and connectivity I believe the real effect has been a closing down of possible ways to approach, interpret, and *be* in the world. In other words, the opening up taking place under globalisation is really the enclosing of the world within the dominant neo-liberal model, a process that Ulrich Beck (1999) has called 'globalism'. This enclosing of the world is in line with the absurd idea that history ended in 1989 and all that remained was to roll out a formally democratic, free market capitalism across the entire globe. Any country that didn't voluntarily engage in the new common sense of privatisation would be forced to do so through military intervention if necessary.

Our current socio-economic condition, and one must add political and cultural condition, can therefore be defined by this increasingly dogmatic rejection of any alternative to the ideology of privatisation and markets that now frames what is deemed to be both legitimate and true. Quite bizarrely this rejection of alternatives takes place in the name of democracy, a topic I will need to return to in the final chapter. Although the so-called 'Arab Spring' indicates the possibility of alternatives it is unclear yet how these uprisings, even if they liberate themselves from the tyranny of autocratic dictatorship, will escape the clutches of the plutocratic oligarchy that disseminates free market dogma around the globe and practices the wholesale enclosure of the commons. If the revolutions result in something more recognisably Western it is certain that liberalisation will be primarily economic. The alter-globalisation movement(s) that have found their most recent expression in the call to occupy Wall Street also present alternatives, and as the international take up of the call indicates this is a cause that can still resonate around the world and arouse significant forms of identification and solidarity. Detractors, however, were quick to point out that the globalising Occupy movement failed to come up with an alternative to neo-liberal capitalism, and it failed not because a properly democratic alternative will necessarily take time to arise from the deliberative practices of those involved, but simply because there isn't one. For years now those with alternative views of society, whether idealist or materialist, have been derided as naïve, sometimes mad, but almost certainly adrift from 'reality', but the enclosure that is taking place today – and one that became evident with the eviction of the occupiers – is one where any kind of radicalism is increasingly equated with criminality, if not terrorism. Today even the poor are regarded as a threat to *security*.

There are always alternatives, of course there are, but the enclosure, marginalisation, or repression of radical choices is regularly secured through the announcement that there are none. In fact, as the financial crisis of 2008 showed, we are tied to the activities and the interests of a capitalist oligarchy to such an extent that the necessary changes to the system would have such far-reaching consequences that change becomes increasingly difficult. Developed countries in particular (where developed increasingly signals the establishment of mature consumer cultures) have been taken so far into the world of financial speculation that finding a way out is increasingly problematic. Our credit-fuelled lifestyles are unsustainable, but it has become the world we know. For the vast majority of people living in the so-called advanced economies credit and the objects and experiences credit supplies have been woven into the fabric of our everyday lives. Given that for the last three decades we have been told that credit is our 'flexible friend' or that as consumers we are sovereign, demanding changes to people's everyday habits and expectations will be justifiably met with considerable resistance. As I will argue below, this imbrication of financial capital into the very tissue of everyday practices has affected who we think we are in the sense that, especially for those born since 1980, it has become part of our very being. This means that thinking about alternatives is more of an ontological problem than an epistemological one. Knowing that the system is deeply flawed doesn't necessarily help me change things, because who I am remains intimately tied to the world in which I live.

Capitalist subjectivity is predicated on the empty signifier of 'choice', a term that can seemingly be attached to anything and increasingly determines how we view economics, politics and culture as arenas for the pursuit of personal satisfaction. This is also mediated by an array of commodities to which our sense of self is increasingly tied. We have come to understand life as a consumerist adventure in which we scroll through various lifestyle options to find the one that best expresses the inner truth of our individuality. Many people might now be aware that this has all been done with an unstable surfeit of credit, but because change will necessarily bring with it the demand to reappraise how we live and who we think we are, which in turn generates profound anxiety, there is a tendency to carry on regardless. As I will show this means identification with a crisis-ridden system cannot be reduced to false consciousness. As I have already said, it is not an epistemological problem. It is not the case that we do not know. It is rather that thinking about the necessary change instigates an ontological disturbance that makes us want to forget that we do know. This problem, however, should not be interpreted as an excuse for resigning ourselves to things as they are, or a political quietism. Quite the contrary, we have to change the way our economy and our society works. The time has come for different ways of thinking and doing beyond the market fundamentalism that has dominated the last 30 years, and has threatened, or in some instances directly brought about social devastation (depending on which part of the world you live in, and to which 'class' you belong), but to do this it is necessary to understand why such an evidently crisis-ridden fundamentalism can still attract us like moths to a flame. This means retaining an element of ideology critique, especially as offered by Louis Althusser, but supplementing this with an ontological analysis, most notably the one developed by Martin Heidegger in *Being and Time* to account for why the irruption of a crisis invariably calls for the reinforcement of the world as it is.

This will be taken up in more detail in the second half of this chapter, but it does raise a couple of other issues about the shape of the book as a whole. Firstly, there is the concern that the free market dogma that privileges the private accentuates this tendency to reinforce the world as it is. Arguably, one of the most important aspects of Heidegger's analysis was the way in which he explained our tendency for closing ourselves off to any radical questioning of the world as it has already been interpreted. As already noted, because our sense of self cannot be separated from the world we inhabit, any challenge to that world is a direct challenge to us. Such a situation invariably leaves us in an extremely vulnerable position from which we try to extricate ourselves by building fortifications against that challenge rather than permitting ourselves to be undone. By giving primacy to the sovereign individual and conferring veracity on the self-interested, socially closed monad current ideology only exaggerates this tendency. Having sought to eradicate any sense of dependency on or responsibility for others our vulnerability has been presented as a communist myth designed to legitimate the increased role of the state. Against this, free market capitalism putatively supports the full flowering of the impervious individual in the socio-economic system best suited to the satisfaction of each and every desire. It is hardly surprising, then, that when the crisis hits and our vulnerability resurfaces it is met with even greater shock and more widespread denial. To this effect the latter part of this chapter uses Heidegger's work to give a more detailed account of this personal denial, while chapters 4 and 5 show how any questioning is socially curtailed through the advent of managerialism and the new technologies of distraction.

This leads, then, on to the second point, namely that it is not my intention in this book to set out an alternative economics but to consider in detail the nature of this dogma and show how it has come to flood the entire social field. As I will argue in chapters 2 and 3 it is an ideology that ruthlessly and relentlessly privileges the private, rendering any reference to the public a heresy, and any use of the public a social evil. The fact that this system only now survives because of an enormous public intervention has rendered any claim that only the private is good entirely spurious. At least it should have. However, as a dogma and an increasingly totalising common sense, the inconsistency or irrationality of the privateers' argument becomes invisible; and it becomes invisible to such an extent that those who benefit most from the current system are able to invert causality and portray the public realm as the problem. Much in keeping with what Naomi Klein (2007) has called 'disaster capitalism' the collapse of the capitalist system has been re-imagined as a failing of big government. Very soon after the crisis became public (at least as measured by discussion on BBC Radio 4's *Today* programme) the discourse very rapidly moved from the greed, recklessness and irresponsibility of bankers, to the need for a public bailout, and then within the course of a few days to the lack of public money, to excessive government spending, and a 'bloated' public sector. While the financial sector remains largely unchanged, a situation that has even orthodox economists bewildered, the public sector is now having wholesale reforms imposed on it.

In the UK, with the election of a Tory government in 2010, it was as if the anti-state party suddenly had its own 9/11. In the way that the events of 11 September 2001 were seized upon by the Bush administration to invade any country it felt it could, the events of 2008 have been seized on by British Conservatives as a once in a lifetime opportunity to complete the privatisation of public services that has been the policy challenge for every British government since Margaret Thatcher, irrespective of their 'right' or 'left' lineage. Options for socio-economic organisation have been closed down to such an extent that a crisis brought about by the privileging of the private and a commitment to deregulation is responded to by further rounds of privatisation and deregulation. For the high priests of the dogma, which includes a range of actors both inside and outside the corporate world, the crisis has in no way interrupted their worldview, but has instead been taken as a further opportunity to extend it. The belief in privatisation has taken on a certain religiosity where no empirical evidence to the contrary can shake the blind faith in market solutions. The aim of this book, therefore, is to give a sense of the implications of this dogma in the areas of economics, politics and culture, but to also show why, despite the attempted closure of alternatives, the world can and will be opened up again.

MARKETS IN EVERYTHING

To get a sense of this dogma's ethos we need only look at what I had assumed was the nadir of this cult, namely the FutureMAP project, dubbed the 'market in death' by indignant US senators who felt uncomfortable about a futures market being used to predict security risks in the Middle East, and terrorist threats potentially becoming a lucrative trade for Wall Street. According to Robin Hanson, 'strategic decisions depend upon the accurate assessment of the likelihood of future events. This analysis often requires independent contributions by experts in a wide variety of fields, with the resulting difficulty of combining the various opinions into one assessment. Market-based techniques provide a tool for producing these assessments' (see hanson.gmu.edu). Although the FutureMAP programme was closed there remains a desire to use futures markets in this way and others have appeared (and continue to appear) that bear a passing resemblance to FutureMAP. However, while profiting from terror might have upset the good taste of US senators, profiting from society's most needy does not seem to generate such a reaction.

Most recently, and despite the collapse of the financial system, the use of Social Impact Bonds in the UK has been floated as a solution to the problems associated with poverty. Pioneered by Social Finance, an organisation created in 2007 to 'build a social investment market in the UK [and] combine a deep understanding of social issues with expertise in financial modelling', Social Impact Bonds continue to be promoted as financial tools designed to pull in money from non-governmental investors for preventative projects aimed at early intervention in issues ranging from mental health, youth offending and re-offending, to school truancy and exclusion. These investments are designed to replace government spending by driving 'significant non-government investment into addressing the causes of deep-rooted social problems with returns generated from a proportion of the related reduction in spending on acute services' (Social Finance 2009:2). Social Impact Bonds thus offer investors the chance to take profits from the differential between what the state would have had to pay for 'crisis interventions', in other words spending money on the effects of poverty later in life, compared to what they save by intervening early using these financial innovations. As Social Finance explains, profits come from a government commitment 'to use a proportion of the savings that result from improved social outcomes to reward non-government investors' (3). Incentive is then built in by giving greater rewards for investments that result in improved social outcomes measured according to pre-agreed metrics. The overall aim, then, is to create a paradigm shift from negative to positive spending cycles, moving away from the 'catch-22' scenario where the high cost of crisis spending results in less resources and less intervention, to more early intervention, less cost, and more resources.

While this all sounds very good there remains the lingering thought that Social Finance has not found a way of helping the poor, but a new way for the rich to benefit from social immiseration; a case of capitalism cannibalising its own waste. This might display some of the benefits of recycling that are *de rigueur* in any right thinking consumer society, but it is more likely the discovery of a new profitable resource, and one can only assume that once this resource has been found the non-governmental investors would not like to deplete it to the point where it no longer sustains profits. While the explosion of the financial sector over the last 30 years has offered numerous new ways for the rich to exploit the poor, with the now infamous sub-prime loans being a perfect example, what is different here is that Social Finance seem to have moved away from the mediation of the mortgage market to a means of directly profiting from the condition of the most disadvantaged. Although the bonds are limited to specific social issues at present it is not clear why the future might not bring a host of Social Impact Bonds facilitating investment in a wide range of social ills enabling the development of complex portfolios of securitised abuse.

The rhetoric of Social Finance is certainly laudable and represents a development of the kind of social intervention that has been part of the philanthropic tradition for a very long time – only with the exception that this is not charitable donation, but for-profit investment – but the incentives seem misguided. Is there not a chance that Social Impact Bonds will start to function in much the same way traditional bond markets function, where low interest rates are paid on bonds from countries deemed to have secure economies, like the US, UK, Japan and Germany, but much higher interest rates are paid on bonds from 'developing' countries that have not yet shown the kind of long-term fiscal and political discipline that earns the trust of investors. Won't we actually see low but stable profits from social immiseration in the UK, and high but unstable profits from bonds taken out in the Third World? A securitised portfolio of social immiseration would then look for continued poverty in the UK with some intervention bringing in low but secure returns, and investment in the developing world where continued social immiseration would reap higher returns for riskier interventions and where the lack of developed public scrutiny would make it easier for governments and investors to collude in order to justify the profits they make. In fact why would investors want social problems to be solved when the further production of social immiseration is a good, long-term investment? It seems counter-productive to want to truly transform the condition of the poor. In this regard what Social Impact Bonds actually represent is a means for investors to profit from the productive management of the poverty capitalism produces. The current system continues to generate poverty as certainly as it produces wealth, but money can now be made from managing the most anti-social or inefficient aspects of poverty in order to create the ideal conditions to maximally exploit immiseration as an investment opportunity. While Social Impact Bonds have been invented to transform the way social outcomes are achieved, the ultimate social outcome will be the most profitable management of poverty, transforming expenditure into income; and this, of course, would be a very important step in the long-term formation of a fully corporate state.

The Social Impact Bond is therefore a very interesting innovation for a number of reasons. As the perfect expression of ideological closure it demonstrates how the private realm is increasingly seen as a solution to all our needs; that it is now perfectly legitimate to see poverty as a profit-making opportunity; and that the role of government is simply to facilitate the pursuit of private profit which is the only means for achieving social well-being, but what is also revealing about Social Impact Bonds is that the UK government is still investigating their use. That Social Impact Bonds might still be seen as a good thing is further evidence of the refusal or inability to think beyond the logic that brought us economic catastrophe. Our current condition is so profoundly disabling that even when its fatality is clearly demonstrated there is no discernable alteration to our thinking and practices. This is a truly fundamentalist position. There is, then, no sense of irony in the claims made by Social Finance that Social Impact Bonds will create 'a rational investment market', or that they will 'align government policy priorities with the interests of non-government investors' (2009:4). Much of our current predicament stems precisely from these two absolutely central issues. The speculative orgy that resulted in the financial crisis issued in the main from the completely fallacious idea that markets are rational, and this was facilitated by the increased alignment between politicians and corporate interests that enabled the marginalisation of any argument to the contrary, and with that the closure of policy decisions.

The task of this book, then, is to set out this enclosure of the socio-economic and political imaginary, and show how the market has become the measure of truth as well as the ultimate arbiter of every social relationship. This dogmatic condition whereby the principles of privatisation – individualism, financialisation, free markets, and commodification – encompass every aspect of life I have chosen to call idiotism. It is at once an ideology or general set of ideas and representations, a set of discursive practices that practically inform a variety of social sites, and a heightening of the ontological closure I have briefly introduced above. In the next two sections I will unpack this ontological moment in a little more detail before setting out the content and structure of the ideology in chapter 2. Chapters 3, 4, and 5 then address idiotism as a discursive practice in the realms of economics, politics and culture, before returning to the work of Heidegger to show how, despite explaining our tendency to turn away from any radical questioning an ontological analysis also shows why resistance and alternatives always remain possible.

IDIOTISM

The term 'idiotism' is derived from the ancient Greek word for the private, *idios* (ιδιος), and to understand how this word might refer to dogma understood more broadly as well as the dogmatic application of privatisation it is important to work through the other meanings associated with it. In the first instance *idios* refers to the personal realm, that which is private, and one's own. It can therefore also be used to refer to private property or personal belongings. As I use the term idiotism it refers to a condition dominated by the belief that the free use and disposal of private property, that is economic freedom, is the necessary condition for civic freedom. This primary meaning of the word *idios* also has the connotation of privacy as that which is enclosed, marking out a border between interior and exterior, thus referring to something distinct and separate. This connotation of enclosure is also present in my use of idiotism because, as already mentioned, the creation of the private through the enclosure of public or commonly held resources has historically been the primary means by which property has been secured for private use. This method still remains the major form of primitive accumulation today as the enclosure of common land continues apace in the Third World, alongside more contemporary forms of enclosure such as the increased patenting of genetic material and bioforms (see Shiva 2000 and 2003). Primarily, then, idiotism signifies the dominance of the private and the securing of further private property through the process of enclosure.

Secondly, this enclosure of the private also enables me to speak of idiotism as a dogma, as that which closes down thinking and practice. Again the Greek word δόγμα means personal or private opinion, and therefore has a strong connection to the *idios*. Dogma has its root in the word δοκέω meaning to think, suppose, or imagine. It also refers to how things seem or appear. The related word δοκῖμος also adds the meaning of something esteemed, authorised, and approved, from where we get our own understanding of doctrine as an approved and authorised way of thinking (and δόγματα as the teachings relating to it). That privatisation has become dogmatic or doctrinal is hard to contradict. Privatisation and the associated practices of deregulation, competition, and marketisation have achieved such ascendancy that it is almost impossible to challenge this discourse without seeming to be out of touch, backward, romantic, or even politically sectarian, unwilling to bend the knee to what John McMurtry calls 'corporate absolutism' (2002:65).

McMurtry's work serves as an excellent analysis of the 'primitive syntax' (93) that organises this dogma. According to him, the ruling equations of this world view are '*Freedom = the Free Market = the Global Corporate System*', and inversely '*Opponents of the Global Corporate System = Opponents of the Free Market = Opponents of Freedom*' (53). However, it is not only the reduction of freedom to the free market that is central to idiotism as a dogma it is the role the term 'market' itself plays within the discourse. McMurtry writes: 'What is not noticed is that the concept itself abolishes from possibility any other kind of market except the one that rules [...]. There is no other market before *the* market, as there is no other god before Yahweh' (91). However, the fathers of the free market have no problem that this might involve devotion. Friedrich Hayek freely likens the contemplation of the free market to religious experience. For him it is 'submission to the impersonal forces of the free market' that has 'made possible the growth of a civilization' (2007:212), and he goes on to write that the necessity of submitting to these forces is better served by the 'humble awe' (212) demanded by religion than any rational understanding. All of which raises the dual question of how legitimate it is to refer to such a system as democratic and how democracy might still be conceived as a public counter to such dogma; questions that I will leave for the final chapter.

However, what is interesting about this dogma is that one doesn't need to be writing from a radical or what might be perceived as a partisan position to be concerned about the ascendancy of this increasingly doctrinal and reductive mind-set. Esteemed economists with a long history of establishment service are voicing their concerns. In his essay-length book, *The Economics of Innocent Fraud*, published just prior to his death, John Kenneth Galbraith notes how the supposedly impersonal term 'the market' has come to stand in for the word capitalism because of the attendant baggage that has historically attached itself to that term: crisis, worker subjugation, exploitation. According to Galbraith, though, the idea that there is no longer capitalism, but only the impersonal market is 'not a wholly innocent fraud' (2009:13). That the market, he continues, 'is subject to skilled and comprehensive management is unmentioned' (14). He then goes on to suggest, just like McMurtry, that calling it 'the Corporate System' would be more appropriate, but: 'Sensitive friends and beneficiaries of the system do not wish to assign definitive authority to the corporation. Better the benign reference to the market' (14). And so the doctrine has established itself and continues to set itself up as the only legitimate form of economic, political and social organisation. It has done so to the point of establishing free market economics as a kind of second nature. We are now all accustomed to using words like 'competition', 'efficiency' and 'choice' in relation to our everyday practices. Framing our everyday speech in this way is, of course, a form of social or cultural enclosure.

This introduction of the idea of innocence (or not) leads us to another significant meaning of *idios*, and how it relates to my use of idiotism is very important. From the *idios* as the realm of the private, the language of ancient Greek also gave us the word *idiotes* (ιδιοτες). This term denotes a private person, but also someone of a private status or station, and it is from this word that we derive the secondary and pejorative meaning of the *idiotes* retained in our contemporary use of the word idiot. Because *idiotes* signifies a private person it also has the meaning of layman, or person without specialist or professional knowledge. It is from here that we have inherited our own understanding of the idiot as someone lacking in specialist or higher learning. The idiot has thus become a person of low, vulgar or common sensibilities, taste and education. But this more recent derivation of *idiotes* meaning what is common should not detract from the primary meaning of the word denoting the private. The pejorative version of the prefix *idio* is part of a broad and deep animosity to that which we have in common, while the positive connotations of *idio* – stemming from the *idios* as also meaning the peculiar and the strange – are reserved for the eccentricities of that very personal and individualistic behaviour we call idiosyncratic, especially when such very singular and peculiar behaviour is taken to be part of aristocratic breeding. Here, idiosyncracy becomes the opposite of what is common, the mark of a radical freedom from social convention and custom, and characteristic of an independent and creative mind. While I do not wish to take issue with idiosyncracies, aristocratic or not, the association of *idiotes* and idiocy with the common must be challenged. In fact to counter the idiotism of our times it is precisely the common that needs reaffirming.

In Patrick McDonagh's excellent study of idiocy he notes that the original meaning of the Greek word *idiotes* was retained in England until at least the fourteenth century when the Court of Chancery would use idiot as a legal term to indicate that someone could only work in a private capacity and was no longer suitable for public office (2008:6). Since then, however, the original meaning has been lost and the pejorative use has come to dominate referring to a range of conditions and characteristics including innocence, imbecility, retardation and disability, all of which at different times have been used to designate a clinical condition justifying exclusion and incarceration. Removing the prejudicial antipathy towards the common from my use of idiotism is essential. If any association with the connotations of stupidity or folly are to be retained, however, these arise precisely from the primacy of the private and the separate, and not the common. Stupidity, in our ordinary use of the term, is understood to be synonymous with not thinking, with not being able to see the outcome of an action, or being so wrapped up in oneself and one's own world as to be unable to imagine anything else. If any sense of stupidity is retained, then, it comes from idiotism signifying the self-enclosure of the private. Having said that I have no intention of using idiotism in this pejorative sense. I will not deny that given the instability of our economic, social and ecological systems, the idea that we should carry on doing what we are doing does seem stupid, but this only serves to show that where idiotism is concerned the issue is not knowledge, or not only knowledge, and that there is an important ontological component here that has serious implications for how we might address idiotism as a condition.

Being knowledgeable or gaining more knowledge does not necessarily permit a person to escape the self-enclosure of their world. Knowledge that organic food, for example, is better for the planet, and that the planet might be undergoing radical climate change that could transform life on earth, does not necessarily stop me from buying cheap food at the supermarket because I also need to pay a mortgage, utility bills, insurance policies, and God knows what else. To some this will indicate a fundamental flaw in my character; a lack of commitment, or lack of courage, perhaps. This might be true, but I would like to argue that I carry on not because I am morally defective, but because I am an idiot. My personal or private concerns press upon me in such a manner so as to make any exit or radical alternative very difficult, and these private concerns become more pronounced precisely in a world that atomises and individualises. The point is, I can easily think otherwise, but something else holds my practice and my world in place.

This requires a couple of important qualifications which will be developed more fully below. Firstly, there is something self-enclosing and self-reproducing about my world and the everyday practices from which it is comprised. The world, despite being made up of self and other, sameness and difference, is relatively closed. In many respects it is predictable, routine and, by definition, habitual. This means that I also use idiotism to refer to a self-generating or self-reproducing system. Ordinarily such reproduction has been addressed via an attention to ideology critique. The work of Althusser is exemplary in this regard. He famously opened his influential study entitled 'Ideology and Ideological State Apparatuses' with the following: 'As Marx said, every child knows that a social formation which did not reproduce the conditions of production at the same time as it produced would not last a year. The ultimate condition of production is therefore the reproduction of the conditions of production' (1984:1). The fact that capitalism had not collapsed beneath the weight of its own contradictions was something that influenced Gramsci's study of hegemony that in turn enabled him to account for the continuation of a system that ought to be too unstable to do so. Althusser inherits and develops Gramsci's thinking in this matter, exploring the function of the ideological apparatuses such as church and school that ensure the continuation of the world as it is. However, this axiom of ideology critique is also very revealing. In the first instance I am not sure that every child knows this. My child knows a lot, especially about superheroes and dinosaurs, but he has not yet explained to me how his primary school is reproducing the conditions for the reproduction of the capitalist system, even though it evidently is. This also means that ideology critique regularly falls prey to the assumption that anyone who isn't aware of how society reproduces itself is worse than infantile, an idiot in the pejorative sense of the word.

Secondly, then, this means that ideology critique tends to overplay the role of knowledge. Another key element in Althusser's essay is that we live out imaginary relations to real conditions. This is part of the critical tradition that has attributed the continuation of capitalism to some form of false consciousness. Again, there is the suggestion that we are all duped, that we are either naively innocent or blindly stupid. Change can therefore only come about through a programme of revelation and re-education, a claim that has profoundly disturbing consequences. The central problem, however, remains this privileging of knowledge. Even if ideology critique refrains from treating people as worse than infantile the privileging of knowledge or some faulty consciousness fails to address how idiotism as a condition has an ontological component that supports its epistemological content. Idiotism certainly is epistemological in the sense that it functions through the deployment of various representations, descriptions and truth claims about human nature and the workings of society. It is also epistemological in that these discourses become common sense and are repeated, reproduced and legitimated by all manner of everyday utterances, gestures and rituals, but the capacity for idiotism to become all-embracing is supported by ontological conditions that tie each and every person into the world they know.

When Althusser spoke about living imaginary relations to real conditions he was certainly presenting an argument about how we come to know ourselves and our world, but the use of the imaginary here did not mean that we live in some kind of fantasy world. Reducing Althusser's use of the imaginary to the conventional understanding of false consciousness does him a serious disservice. In evoking the imaginary Althusser was addressing the psychological and ontological function of ideology. In this sense ideology becomes a functional system that 'recruits' subjects' (48) through a wide variety of practices and rituals. Here, Althusser is directly borrowing from the work of Jaques Lacan to account for the way in which ideology reproduces any given system by enabling the recognition of our place within it. Again, this does not aim to show how we are duped into thinking and acting in particular ways, but how our identity is tied up with the social system into which we are born, and the practices and rituals that enable that system to reproduce itself.

In Lacanian psychoanalysis the imaginary is an important stage in subjective development whereby the infant's nascent sense of subjectivity emerges out of its relationship with the image of another person that the child assumes as its own. This phase in psychological development was in turn borrowed from Hegel and stages a reformulation of his struggle for recognition between the master and the slave that Hegel presents as the motor of History. The brilliance of Hegel was to formulate the idea that humans ought to be understood in terms of negativity rather than any predetermined positive content that would secure their identity before the fact. Without any pregiven identity humans variously posit identities that require validation through a process of recognition. Identity formation is thus inherently social as each 'I' is dependent on another to affirm the identity it has assumed. Such an identity is inherently unstable, but such instability can be overcome by regular and persistent rituals and practices that confirm who we are. For Hegel, lack of recognition undoes the subjectivity assumed and violence will often ensue from such a crisis. The social experience of this would be those individuals or groups who refuse to adopt and thereby confirm the subjectivity that wider society has chosen to assume. Such individuals and groups are seen as threats to social stability, making another key function of ideology the construction of delinquency, criminality, or perversion. The point being that none of these are epistemological categories. Instead they point to a deeply ontological component in the success of any ideology, and it is this ontological component in addition to the content of the ideology that idiotism highlights.

Returning to Althusser, he argues that the ideological recognition function is that which produces 'the "obviousness" that you and I are subjects' (1984:47). It also produces the effect which he terms 'the practical *denegation* of the ideological character of ideology [...]: ideology never says, 'I am ideological' (49). This recognition function that he also calls 'interpellation' is the function that thoroughly binds us to our world, and it does so through innumerous rituals and practices that hold us in place even when we know otherwise. This is why knowledge and the explanation of false consciousness are entirely inappropriate. My subjectivity is tied into my world to such an extent that changes to my world demand radical changes to my subjectivity that are not easily or readily achievable. The idea that 'I' am separate from my world and can choose my 'lifestyle' is in fact a cornerstone of idiotism. Very often alternatives are not so much genuine alternatives as permutations of the recognition function: idiotism as a condition has become ever more sensitive to the productivity and profitability of a plethora of personal life-style choices all modelled on some ideal Subject.

In this regard, Althusser argued that religion best exemplifies the recognition function. He writes that the

> 'procedure' to set up Christian religious subjects is dominated by a strange phenomenon: the fact that there can only be such a multitude of possible religious subjects on the absolute condition that there is a Unique, Absolute, *Other Subject*, i.e. God. [...] It then emerges that the interpellation of individuals as subjects presupposes the 'existence' of a Unique and central Other Subject, in whose Name the religious ideology interpellates all individuals as subjects. (52–3)

He goes on to say, after Lacan, that the 'Unique and Absolute Subject is *specular*' (54): God is Subject and all his subjects are '*reflections*' (53) of him. With respect to our current condition it might be said that we are made after the image of the big idiot in the sky. God is the ultimate example of the *idiotes*. He works in mysterious (idiomatic) ways through the free use and disposal of his personal property, which extends to the entirety of creation. He alone is separated from it as sole creator. Having mixed his labour with the *tehom* to give form to all things he became the proprietor of all that is. Present everywhere yet separated off God is the private Subject to which all other private subjects aspire. It is thus hardly surprising that religion sits so well with many, if not all, advocates of capitalism.

THE ONTOLOGY OF IDIOTISM

While Althusser helps us think about the enclosure and reproduction of a system in terms that are ontological rather than purely epistemological there are problems with this approach, not least the apparent lack of agency or history. It has been the source of much perplexity that Althusser should be a Marxist and yet in this essay offer an account of ideology that seems so self-perpetuating as to leave no room for manoevre. In order to draw out the issue of how some change, confrontation or challenge might be incorporated into a seemingly closed system it will be necessary to consider another approach taken from the work of Heidegger. In his analysis of the relationship between human beings – for which Heidegger preferred to use the term 'Dasein' – and the worlds they live in we are offered a philosophy that assists with the examination of the ontological underpinnings of contemporary idiotism. However, because Dasein is defined as *the being for whom its being is an issue*, this is also a hermenuetic analysis. In other words, because it places the role of interpretation and contestation very much at the heart of the human condition, it also offers a means for thinking the resistance and possibilities for change that I will address in the final chapter. For now, though, I would like to introduce the element most in keeping with the idea of systemic reproduction and dogmatic closure, but one that takes us beyond issues of epistemology and false consciousness. This is the condition Heidegger called 'absorption', a concept that also requires some correction of Heidegger's own prejudice towards the public.

To properly understand what Heidegger means by the term Dasein, literally translated as being-there, some discussion is required of what he understands by the term world. Importantly, Dasein is always in-the-world and cannot *be* otherwise. It might be said there is an attachment between ourselves and our world that explains why we can't just *think* ourselves out of it. The world is our home in a way that exceeds volition, choice and decision. To address this fully, however, it is necessary to note the specific way Heidegger uses ontology. For Heidegger, the usual understanding of the world thought in terms of objects and objectivity is an ontic rather than properly ontological understanding. Although Hannah Arendt (1958) was well aware of the distinction, the ontic is in keeping with her use of the term in *The Human Condition*, where various objects that are the product of human work carry, display or epitomise the values of a given community or society. Such things then produce an objective world that mediates between people and endures over time. In contrast to the world of material and ideational things an ontological conception of the world speaks of a primary characteristic of human being itself: world doesn't indicate something objectively distinct from the subject, but indicates a fundamental characteristic of human existence, or, indeed, *how* human beings *are*.

In an early lecture series published under the title *Phenomenological Interpretations of Aristotle*, Heidegger introduces the term world as a phenomenological category that 'immediately names [...] *what* is lived, the content aimed at in living, that which life holds to' (2001:65). Here Heidegger still adheres to some element of the ontic understanding of a world as a *what*, but he is already attempting to show that human life cannot be separated from a sense of the world. Living, for humans, is always, and can only be living *as* something or *for* something. There is no human life that makes sense outside of its world. Thus life always has the structure of 'being in, out of, for, with, and against a world' (65). This means life and world are intimately related, but not as 'two separate self-subsistent Objects' (65). In Division I of *Being and Time* Heidegger calls this structure the 'primary datum' (1996:49). Dasein should be understood '*a priori* as grounded upon that constitution of being which we call *being-in-the-world*' (49), which is to be taken as a whole and must not be split up. This is why he doesn't use the term human being with its connotations of objective presence. For Heidegger, the presupposition of an object-subject split 'is truly fatal' (55) for philosophy. This also means that being-in must not be understood in a spatial sense. It is not 'objective presence "in" something objectively present' (50) like water in a glass, or a dress in a closet, to take Heidegger's examples. If you take the dress out of the closet it is still a dress. Dasein, however, can't be separated from the world. Ontically, Dasein can certainly be understood as being surrounded by objects and things, or living in particular environments. Dasein can thus be said to live within specific 'worlds', i.e. regions of objects, tools and practices that distinguish the mathematical 'world' from the legal 'world', or the 'world' of dance from the 'world' of war, but being-in must also be understood ontologically as *how* we are. In other words, we can't *be* otherwise. In the language of the early lecture series, life always refers to a world and this referentiality is always acutalised in life. This is the basic *fact* of our existence. In Heidegger's language this is the *facticity* of Dasein, and such facticity is crucial for understanding the lure of dogmatism.

According to this understanding life is also always lived within a certain inheritance and is moved in a certain direction; always operating within a given history and with certain possibilities in view. Dasein is thus always historically framed. Post-history is alien to Dasein. The particular world in which Dasein takes up home is what Heidegger calls a referential totality, where each thing, idea, or practice makes sense and has its use only with reference to other things, ideas and practices. For Heidegger there is no such thing as *a* useful thing, only a totality of useful things. Each individual thing contains a *reference* or *assignment* to something else: useful things belong to other useful things (64) and all are structured and arranged according to the 'what for' and 'in order to', i.e. a set of reasons, aims, meanings and values that organise their relation to each other. These are in turn arranged according to specific ideals, practical objectives and ends that refer to the ultimate 'for the sake of', i.e. Dasein's questioning of itself and its interpretation of what is good and what is right. According to this understanding even the physical attachment of one thing to another, like the board attached to a wall in a classroom, only exists because of the environment in which it appears. Even at the ontic level understanding the world as a referential totality already challenges the conception of self-subsistent objects. All this means that a 'definite manner of Dasein's *having-been-interpreted* stands at its disposal' (2001:25). The world is always already taken 'as' something, and this 'as structure' does not need to be learned but is integral to Dasein's sense of 'self'. What Heiddegger calls the 'as structure' (1996:141) is another way to understand the world that directs Dasein and produces a sense of being-at-home. Thinking this 'as-structure' in relation to current dogma idiotism is that condition whereby the human is understood *as* a self-maximizing, possessive individual operating within a referential totality geared towards competition and private gain. Everything ultimately refers to the market and its efficient functioning.

However, what is important for understanding the seduction of dogma is that this as-structure has a 'disturbable familiarity' (74), perfectly encapsulated in Heidegger's analysis of tools. We are so comfortable with the tools we use, he argues, that we remain largely unaware of them as long as they do what they are assigned to do, only bursting into our consciousness when they breakdown – the pen that runs out of ink, the bike that loses its chain. This also applies to the world more generally. For the majority of the time the world is unproblematic. We go about our everyday dealings with things often without a thought, and the world only 'appears' when something disturbs its regular rhythms and patterns. The fact that what we are familiar with can be disturbed clearly has potential when trying to articulate the need for change, but what is important about Heidegger's analysis is that disturbance to our world can also commit us to engage even more strenuously with what we know and what we ordinarily do. This is because any breakdown in the system of references and assignments can induce an experience of profound anxiety. As each useful thing is tied to every other useful thing a break in any one of them can bring about a chain reaction in the entire system. Because each element in the system is a bearer of significance there is potential for the world of references and assignments to collapse into meaninglessness.

This is most readily perceptible when we lose a loved one and our world just seems to 'fall apart', but the point here is that we do not need to suffer the loss of a loved one for the world to lose its meaning. The malfunctioning of even a minor point of reference can lead beyond the problematising of the task at hand to the entire world manifesting itself as something obtrusive, overburdening and even intolerable. This is because, as noted above, the relevance of useful things ultimately leads back to our sense of who we are. In other words, a tool that breaks down can simply get in the way of the smooth running order of our immediate environment or depending on the context of this breakdown it could lead directly to reflection upon one's being-in-the-world as a whole. Because, for Heidegger, there is no ultimate foundation beyond the meanings we posit and the worlds we create any breakdown of the world's significance can become a breach in the entire edifice of established meaning, which for most people is a profoundly disturbing experience. Ordinarily, such questioning is held in abeyance by the world in which we are absorbed. Absorption in the everyday world of routines and habits functions so as to hold off the self-questioning that might otherwise be incessant. Thus when the world becomes problematic it is not something I can simply respond to as a detached spectator. The problematised world is invariably a problematised 'self'. This is why a purely epistemological view of common sense needs to be countered. Although I might project possibilities for myself that are based on conscious decisions, the world itself is not something I am free to either take up or refuse. 'I' am inextricably bound to 'my' world, wrapped up in it in a way that radically undermines the idea that I assume it only after a period of deep reflection, or am somehow duped into believing this is the way things are.

While Heidegger unequivocally argues that Dasein is world-creating this is never a mastery of the world because Dasein must be understood as the '*dependency of being referred*' (81). This dependency is absolutely crucial as it completely contradicts the tradition of autonomy and *in*dependence that has become the model for the self-contained or self-sufficient individual so integral to the marketised view of life. That which is supposedly indivisible is clearly divided or rather splintered across a complex range of social, political and cultural references in such a manner that should those references be broken, that entity we refer to as the 'subject' is cut adrift searching for the first point to anchor itself again. While we might understand ourselves as sovereign we are in fact wholly dependent on an interpretation of the world that, through the liturgy of the dominant discourse and the regular performance of innumerable practices, has gained a semblance of solidity. This means that disturbance to any world and the threat of meaningless-ness more readily compels us to reaffirm our world by finding solace in the everyday practices that had sustained us up to that point, or to rebuild the world's significance by eradicating that which we believe to be the cause of the threatened dissolution. Hence when the system of privatisation and deregulation collapses we blame the lack of money on a bloated public sector and unnecessary public spending, thereby rescuing the referential totality of privatisation from being undermined. The point to note here is that our first heading when set adrift by a crisis is the shortest course back to where we came from. For Heidegger, the primary response to crisis is not to accept it, learn from it and find an alternative, but to hysterically re-bulid what has fallen apart.

One reason why belief in Fate or God is so strong is because irrespective of the accident that befalls us faith in God's will or resignation to the workings of Fate allow our world to accommodate all things. This is why dogma can have such a hold. If we are to revolutionise our world we invariably need another one in which to feel secure, and nothing is more comforting than a set of teachings to which all thought and action should refer. A problem that Heidegger himself fell prey to. This is often why the dogmas of liberalism and neo-liberalism are countered by the dogmas of communism, socialism, communitarianism, multiculturalism, anarchism or indeed any other political model. The homelessness of freedom is practically impossible for Dasein to bear. In many respects the relationship between Dasein and its world, or Dasein's environment (*Umwelt*) is very much like the closed or autopoietic system of cybernetics. Conceiving of the world as a referential totality is important because the implications give us a clear insight into our ontological vulnerability and our tendency for becoming wrapped up in the comforting dogma that preserves the environment that in turn sustains us.

This absorption, however, is something that Heidegger found deeply troubling because, according to him, it alienates Dasein from the essential questioning that defines it. I will return to this in chapters 5 and 6, but for now it is necessary to address Heidegger's linking of this absorption to his understanding of the public. While Heidegger described the realm of everyday life as a 'levelling down' (1996:157) and a 'falling prey' (164) to the world as it is already given (the 'as-structure' of the world) he protestated that he didn't wish his account of everyday discourse to be seen as 'disparaging' (1996:157). While everyday life remained the necessary ground from which to project an authentic life, and was essential to Dasein's questioning of itself, there remains a strong sense that being 'given over' to publicly accepted ways of thinking and doing – Heidegger uses the term überantwortet – is very much an infantilising operation and is a rendering of the everyday that I would have to contest. I would prefer to stay with the idea that everyday practices remain essential for any future interpretation of the world and be critical of specific types of public discourse rather than public discourse per se.

Heidegger names the 'subject' of this everydayness *das Man*, which is regularly translated as 'the "They"' (107), but could easily be transcribed using the counter-cultural term 'the Man', which has similar connotations of anonymity and authority suggested in Heidegger's usage. Our being-in-the-world as a being-with-others means that 'who' we are is primarily determined by the specific public interpretation that holds sway at any given historical conjuncture. This is a condition whereby we share the same pleasures, taste, information, and world-view as others. For Heidegger the common sense of 'the "They"' frames our dealings with the world as well as the future each singular Dasein might project for itself. It is in this context that Heidegger himself uses the term idiotism. In volume 70 of the *Gesammtausgabe* entitled *Über den Anfang* Heidegger discusses it in relation to the complementary condition of 'planetarism' (*Planetarismus*), which is the global 'equalising' of all of humanity, and defines idiotism in the following way:

> 'Idiotism' is not meant in the psychiatric sense of a limiting of the spirit and the soul, but a definition of that historical condition, the consequence of which is everyone everywhere and at all times has their ἴδιον – their ownmost self [*Eigenes*] recognised as the same as the ownmost selves [*Eigenen*] of all the others and carried out either willingly or unknowingly. The unconditional, being-historical essence of the They is: idiotism. (2005:34–5)

While idiotism as I am using it certainly carries with it the sense of a global reduction of what it means to be human to the model of the possessive individual it is important, as noted above, to avoid this pejorative and derived equation of idiotism with what is held in common or is public. Any criticism of idiotism should focus on the extension of the ideology of private enclosure rather than primarily complain about a supposed public sameness. Idiotism is certainly the generalised privatisation of life that atomises people as self-interested individuals, but it is evidence of Heidegger's own residual individualism (his conservatism) that this results in a complaint about the nature of what is public.

At stake here are two basic understandings of the term public that are almost diametrically opposed. In the first place public denotes something that is used by all. In this sense public refers to something everyone knows or has access to, something that involves the greatest number of people, which for thinkers like Heidegger always translates into mediocrity and sameness. In line with this usage, public represents what is most widely understood, the most broadly accepted world-view, and the dominant ideology. This relationship to ideology is important because what is public for Heidegger is not something derived from reflection, but what is always already familiar to us as our world. It is manifested in all kinds of speech-acts, gestures, and discursive practices, and exemplified by institutional decision and procedure. Contrary to this notion of the public as the most prevalent or most widely accepted there is the definition that also involves that which is shared, but here it pertains to questions regarding how we should live together or understand our condition as being-with-others.

In Richard Polt's (2007) review of Heidegger's unpublished and secret wartime writings he shows that because our being-in-the-world is always a being-with-others, Heidegger had a very clear understanding that Dasein's essential questioning of itself necessarily meant a questioning of the people or community to which Dasein belonged. There is then a strong sense in Heidegger that Dasein's authenticity, that is, Dasein facing up to the question essential to it, was always already a public question, and that the polemical nature of Dasein's interrogation of itself could never be an entirely closed off individuated experience. The public in this sense is therefore always a site of disagreement and confrontation over the dominant interpretation of the world. Heidegger's conservatism would perhaps more readily reserve this sense of the public for the special group of poets and thinkers of which he was so fond, but this suffers from the same critique that most anti-democratic positions suffer from. Staying with Heidegger's own analysis, while remaining entangled in the world or being-at-home is preferable to the anxiety that comes from a sense of our home slipping away, because the essence of Dasein is to question itself 'not-being-at-home must be conceived existentially and ontologically as the more primordial phenomenon' (1996:177); and because this always involves an interpretation of the shared references that make up the world as it is given, this questioning can only be public in the second sense of the term. It is only Heidegger's residual subjectivism that permits him to reduce the public to the notion of averageness and the tranquillity of being absorbed in what we already know.

In the first sense of the term public, idiotism can be said to exaggerate our absorption in the world by closing down, or rather closing off this second, hermeneutic understanding of the public realm as the site for the conflict and contestation of interpretations. When public discourse becomes dominated by the concepts of the individual and the private; when the workings of Dasein are directed through the consumption of commodities; where possibilities are projected only in the display of such commodities' sign value; when our being-with is completely atomised, or at most restricted to family members, we are increasingly deflected away from alternatives, deflected away from butting up against a world that sets ours into relief and begins the reflective process of world creation or re-invention. Put another way, idiotism encourages reflection, but only in the way that a looking glass reflects back my own image. What idiotism works against is any refraction of the light that might cause me to question the image I have of myself and the world that sustains me. However, as I will show in the final chapter, while idiotism seeks to close off the public realm understood in the second sense by reducing it to the reproduction of private concerns it cannot enclose it completely because our hermeneutic condition persists.

Writing in the spring of 2012 there are a host of 'democratic' movements that offer evidence of this persistent struggle over the world as it is given. To what extent the movements loosely collected together under the umbrella of the 'Arab Spring' will become caught up in new formations of nationalism or sectarianism, or are appropriated by the global market system is yet to be seen. What they give credence to, however, is the idea that what is truly democratic is the irruption of a different interpretation of the world within a specific formation of power. That this democratic expression is quite alien to the formal democracy that will seek to claim, capture, regulate and tame it is something that many democratic commentators overlook. In this regard the final chapter will return to the hermeneutic character of our being-in-the-world to address a conception of democracy understood primarily as a challenge to the world as it is given. This address to democracy is necessary because even though idiotism as the dogma of privatisation demands an alternative socio-economic vision founded on our commonality, I am also concerned not to lose sight of the fact that idiotism also represents a general tendency to dogmatic closure and to becoming all wrapped up in the world, a condition exaggerated by idiotism's promotion of privatisation and the possessive individual. This means that any critique of idiotism necessarily demands a critique of the market system, but it also requires us to think beyond equally dogmatic alternatives we might turn to in the search for a different way of being together. The human condition is regularly understood in terms of the reflective capacity that has enabled us to dominate through our use of reason and technology, and yet there is a profound vulnerability to the human condition that also comes from this ability to reflect upon the nature of the world we live in. This vulnerability also, and rather unfortunately, gives us a proclivity for the sort of dogmatic closure that supposedly puts an end to the potentially disturbing questioning that our reflective freedom opens up. Ultimately, while this book focuses on the ideological practices of idiotism as the dogma of privatisation it is with the issue of dogma itself that it concludes. There is no single solution to the problem, no privileged counter to the current totalitarianism, but there is hope that we can live in a world that does not enclose human freedom according to a single interpretation but celebrates its openness, despite the anxieties that may accompany such anarchy.

2
The Ideology of Idiotism

It is generally accepted that the founding father of free market economics is Adam Smith. It is his work that remains the foundation stone for the ideology of idiotism. While I will return to remarks already made about the structure of ideology at the end of this chapter it is important to spend some time here setting out the content of this particular world view in order to understand and contest its basic axioms. Smith's book *An Inquiry into the Nature and Causes of the Wealth of Nations* was first published in 1776, the same year the United States of America declared its independence and established free enterprise as a cornerstone of its civil religion. Smith's book, like all great works, transcended the boundaries of the academy and the discipline of economics that was its primary focus to establish itself in the popular consciousness. To this extent it can be reduced to two famous words: 'invisible hand'. With this phrase Smith was able to tap into the deep-rooted religiosity of a secular discipline and give the free market a near divine status in the economic and political thought that was to follow. Although writing as a man steeped in the tradition of scientific enlightenment Smith nevertheless presented a view of economics with deeply theological overtones. As will be noted when returning to the structure of ideology, at a time in which the assumed natural order of things was being challenged on a number of levels the idea the market reflected a hidden harmony would have resonated with great power.

Two of the key passages from *Wealth of Nations* that have become central to the ideology of idiotism discuss the importance of the pursuit of self-interest as the path to both the furtherance of those private interests *and* the interests of society as a whole. In Book I, in the course of bemoaning the fact that humans are almost the only beings who, once they reach maturity, fail to achieve full independence, he writes: 'man has almost constant occasion for the help of his brethren, and it is in vain for him to expect it from their benevolence only. He will be more likely to prevail if he can interest their self-love in his favour, and shew that it is for their own advantage to do for him what he requires of them. [...] It is not from the benevolence of the butcher, the brewer, or the baker, that we expect our dinner, but from their regard to their own interest' (1998:22). Here it is capitalist self-love rather than a collectivist love of others that is the prime mover and social regulator. Secondly, in Book Four, the 'invisible hand' passage reads as follows:

> As every individual [...] endeavours as much as he can both to employ his capital in the support of domestick [private] industry [...]; every individual necessarily labours to render the annual revenue of the society as great as he can. He generally, indeed, neither intends to promote the publick interest, nor knows how much he is promoting it. By preferring the support of domestick [...] industry, he intends only his own security [... but is] led by an invisible hand to promote an end which was no part of his intention. [...] I have never known much good done by those who affected to trade for the publick good. (291–2)

In this passage the priority of the pursuit of private concerns is once more privileged, but importantly for idiotism it makes a central claim regarding the dangers of directly and intentionally pursuing what might be deemed the public good.

However, what has not been handed down as part of the popular digest of *Wealth of Nations* is the point at which Smith directly contradicts himself and sets out in much detail precisely how and why the public good should be pursued. The fact that he had earlier published an influential book on moral sentiments has always been something of a problem for the ideological purists who wish to reduce everything to the functioning of the free market, and Book V of *Wealth of Nations* introduces further difficulties for the most doctrinaire of free marketeers. Interestingly enough this problem emerges directly out of the principle method of social organisation that is almost universally recognised by orthodox economists as contributing to the greatest wealth and advancement of nations, namely the division of labour. This mode of organisation is of such importance to Smith that it is the subject of the first chapter of Book I. As far is it can be deployed, this method of social organisation, he argues, will 'occasion, in every art, a proportional increase of the productive powers of labour' (13). It creates particular talents, as people find it is in their interest to pursue a particular line of productivity or service that is in demand. The division of labour, however, is insufficient on its own. It needs to be accompanied by the ability to barter and exchange in order to bring the differing talents to fruition and fully develop social productivity. It is peculiar to humans to do this. For Smith, different breeds of dogs with their varying talents are unable to get together to tackle a problem more swiftly or more efficiently because they lack the capacity to barter and exchange.

In the natural world, then, the pursuit of a very rigid, fixed, or closed self-interest is very limiting, if not entirely counter-productive. Here then is the first problem for the ideology of the private. The division of labour pre-supposes a sense for co-operation and of social roles. Indeed, for Smith the division of labour emerges out of this prior sociality. Smith's self-interest is not absolute but premised upon a sense of social need, or doing what the existing social organisation suggests is the best thing to do. The person in a tribe who makes bows and arrows does so in pursuit of his own self-interest, but this possibility only emerges out of his relations with other members of the tribe, and by extension with other tribes. This may appear a very technical point, but the status of the collective is at stake here. As we will see, the collective is driven out of free market analysis by Smith's twentieth-century followers, but in Smith himself, if we read it carefully, the collective and the social are a priori conditions for the emergence of individual talents. It is certainly not something that can be cut away to leave the purity of private interests standing in the full glory of their independence. In fact what emerge as economic roles stem from already existing social roles that purely economic functions can never transcend.

What is more, the opening analysis of the division of labour also shows Smith to be something of a social constructionist, which is an undoubted problem for his more conservative disciples. While all capitalists would argue that one of the wonders of the system is its capacity to foster social mobility there are many who argue that a person's position in the social hierarchy is determined by natural talent. Those who are unsuccessful – which today only means poor – are so due to an unfortunate, but innate lack of talent, if not laziness. That Smith should maintain that the division of labour is a result of functional differentiation within society and is not to be taken as the marker of natural divisions premised on talents inherent in individuals from birth is interesting because it raises the issue of respect for, and equality of occupations that tend to be more central to collectivist or socialist theories of social organisation. On the 'natural talents' Smith remarks that the difference between individuals is actually 'much less than we are aware of; and the very different genius which appears to distinguish men of different professions, when grown up to maturity, is not upon many occasions so much the cause, as the effect of the division of labour. The difference between the most dissimilar characters, between a philosopher and a common street porter, for example, seems to arise not so much from nature, as from habit, custom, and education' (23–4). Had this come from a Marxist treatise on equality of occupation it would not seem out of place. One can only surmise from this passage, then, that if the talents emerging at maturity are the effect of the division of labour, what other talents, characteristics and dispositions are the effect of our mode of social organisation? In many respects self-interest and competition can only be assumed as primary and pre-social if some artificial firewall is built between these traits and other socially moulded characteristics.

If these two issues are only suggestive of problems when advocating the division and free exchange of labour and its products, Smith is absolutely adamant in Book V of *Wealth of Nations* that the division of labour can be so detrimental to society in one important respect that intervention on behalf of the state, or Sovereign, is actually imperative. Book V is interesting for two directly related reasons: the first is that it contains Smith's arguments for the nature and necessity of public works, and secondly, despite this book being almost a quarter of the complete text, it is the book that is most readily excised in the varying abridged versions. There is something about Book V that is very un-Smith-like, but this is only because the Adam Smith we have come to know and love has been effectively divorced from any suggestion that public works are either worthwhile or necessary. Much in the way he has been divorced from his earlier work on morality. Of the three areas demanding public intervention that Smith sets out, the first two will be found in even the most ardent of privateers' writings: the military and the courts of law. Every society requires the monopoly on violence secured by the sovereign to protect against civil war and foreign invasion. Related to this, every society also requires that the state uphold the principles of law and justice. Every society requires legislation and an executive power with the capacity to enforce it. However, in addition to this Smith adds education as the third of his public works describing it in terms of the 'attention of government [...] necessary in order to prevent the almost entire corruption and degeneracy of the great body of the people' (429). What is interesting here is that education, for Smith, ought not be primarily concerned with maximising the talents produced by the division of labour, but actually countering the damaging effects of it. On considering the different types of education for the different 'orders of the people' he writes the following:

> In the progress of the division of labour, the employment [...] of the great body of the people, comes to be confined to a few very simple operations [...] The man whose whole life is spent in performing a few simple operations, of which the effects too are, perhaps, always the same, or very nearly the same, has no occasion to exert his understanding, or to exercise his invention in finding out expedients for removing difficulties which never occur. He [...] becomes as stupid and ignorant as it is possible for a human creature to become. [...] His dexterity at his own trade seems, in this manner, to be acquired at the expense of his intellectual, social, and martial virtues. But [...] this is the state into which the labouring poor, that is, the great body of the people, must necessarily fall, unless government takes some pains to prevent it. (429)

Surprisingly, this quote could be used in support of a Marxist critique of alienation and certainly condemns the Taylorist principles so integral to capitalism's industrial phase. For Smith, then, the division of labour and the free market did bring into being the most complex and wealthy societies, but, in his view, if left entirely without intervention they were also capable of producing a level of social degeneracy and ignorance that outstripped even the so-called barbarous societies. It might be argued that the free market has found its own solution to this problem through the use of regular redundancy and the demand to retrain, thereby lifting people out of what Smith regarded as the stupor of repetition and the comfort of habit. The point, however, is not whether we agree with Smith on the type of intervention necessitated by the social relations of free market capitalism. Despite believing the division of labour supported by a system of free enterprise and exchange was the best of systems, he still believed that some form of intervention *was* required. Unlike contemporary idiotism, which claims the work of Smith for itself, he had his questions and his concerns about such a system. By contrast idiotism has expunged any and every doubt. It has become a purified, unblinking faith in the messianic qualities of the free market liberated from any trace of public intervention, governance, or regulation beyond the juridical-military function. The free circulation and exchange of private property is all that is

required, and that path to contemporary idiotism began with the
work of Friedrich Hayek.

THE DANGERS OF COLLECTIVISM

In the introduction to *The Road to Serfdom* Hayek writes: 'If in the
long run we are the makers of our own fate, in the short run we are
the captives of the ideas we have created' (2007:58). Writing in 1944
and anticipating a postwar world where Britain, the country in which
he was exiled, would be required to rejuvinate itself economically,
politically and culturally, Hayek was concerned that the British
people were becoming too accustomed to the collectivism necessary
for the war effort. His book was intended to recapture the spirit of
individual liberty that British philosophers (including Adam Smith)
had done so much to contribute to in the past and challenge the idea
that collectivism would need to be retained when the immediate
necessity for it had passed. 'There exists now', he continued, 'the
same determination that the organization of the nation which has
been achieved for the purposes of defense shall be retained for the
purposes of creation' (58). But what was required, he asserted, was
the 'intellectual courage' (59) to admit that collectivism, other than
at a time of dire emergency, is wrong. There is no greater tragedy,
he warns, than the pursuit of our highest ideals unintentionally
bringing about the opposite of what we seek. For Hayek the enemy
that Britain was then facing would become its fate if it continued
to be enthralled by the collectivist spirit. His argument was that
an organised economy leads to an authoritarian society, and the
collectivist pursuit of the Good can only bring about the evils of
National Socialism. Collectivism, especially the institutionalised
version we call socialism, is the enemy of freedom according to
Hayek. He feared that amongst the sacrifices and the hardships of
the war socialism as an ideology was benefitting from the enforced
practicalities of wartime collectivism. This meant that while we
were fighting to remain free we were at the same time building our
road to serfdom.

In the opening chapter, dramatically entitled 'The Abandoned
Road', Hayek sums up the situation as follows:

> For at least twenty-five years before the specter of totalitarianism
> became a real threat, we had been progressively moving away
> from the basic ideas on which Western civilization has been built.
> That this movement on which we have entered with such high

hopes and ambitions should have brought us face to face with the totalitarian horror has come as a profound shock to this generation, which still refuses to connect the two facts. Yet this development merely confirms the warnings of the fathers of the liberal philosophy which we still profess. We have progressively abandoned that freedom in economic affairs without which personal and political freedom has never existed in the past. (67)

Liberalism, then, privileges the individual and its freedom. It is 'respect for the individual man *qua* man, that is, the recognition of his own views and tastes as supreme in his own sphere' (68). This is very much in keeping with the philosophical tradition that posits the autonomous subject as the foundation of morality, politics and law, and hence economic activity. This means that the capacities of human reason for spontaneous creation and deliberate reflection exemplify the independence of thought and deed that must be protected and nurtured if man is to be fully human. In light of this, liberalism, for Hayek, goes beyond any 'stationary creed' tied down by hard and fast rules, and is the best possible way to make use of 'the spontaneous forces of society' (71). Hence Hayek's fear concerning the enculturation of the wartime mentality and the two social and political pillars of organisation and collectivism. If these remain part of the postwar psyche Britain will have exchanged the liberal principle of freedom from coercion for the socialist principle of freedom from necessity, which for Hayek is no freedom at all.

Reading Hayek today becomes very interesting if one is in any way sensitive to the ways in which market liberalism has become increasingly dogmatic, if not fundamentalist. The fears that authoritarianism was on the horizon even with a successful completion to the war for the allies has turned out to be very true. The only difference is that the authoritarianism that currently dominates our lives is very much based in the tradition that Hayek claimed to be advocating. The problem – a problem seemingly endemic to economics as a discipline, or at least its neo-liberal strain – is that in pursuit of both economic purity as the best defence against tyranny, and the desire to operate as if it is a *natural* science it has emptied itself of both the philosophy and sociology that would make it the rigorous *social* science it should be. The sort of economics that still has a stranglehold over the discipline today makes all sorts of claims about the human condition and human behaviour, as well as asserting a host of principles pertaining to the socio-political realms, but in fact it has very little to say about any of these things.

Orthodox economics has spent so much effort attaining the kind of rarified abstraction that justifies it basic axioms, as I will show in chapter three, that it has very little basis in the actuality of human existence and human relations. The result has been that in the last few decades the promotion of the pure form of market liberalism has had very little to do with resisting authoritarianism and by contrast has had very close dealings with dictatorship and tyranny, especially in South America (Klein 2007). Recent liberal practice, then, is a far cry from the idealism of Hayek.

The fact that market liberalism is in the end comfortable with dictatorships is because it has such a scant regard for political freedom. By arguing that political freedom is derivable only from the securing of economic freedom – something evident in Hayek, but even more pronounced in the work of Milton Friedman – it fails to understand the dogmatic and authoritarian potential of its own thinking, refusing as it does to properly interrogate or think through the implications of its basic premise. In Hayek this stems from his argument regarding the totalitarian dangers of collectivism; a condition where '*every* activity must derive its justification from a conscious social purpose' (2007:177). For Hayek, of course, as for other liberals in the classic tradition, 'individual freedom cannot be reconciled with the supremacy of one single purpose to which the whole of society must be entirely and permanently subordinated' (213). In this regard the market, based on the free use and disposal of one's private property, is assumed to act as a barrier to the imposition of any such single purpose. As a formal system of exchange amongst free and supposedly equal individuals the market is claimed to be the most suitable ground out of which a more extended notion of freedom can grow. However, what Hayek fails to recognise is that for anything to be supported by a free market within a capitalist system it can only survive by securing a profit, which thereby achieves the supremacy of a single social purpose. It cannot be doubted that anything unable to run at a profit within a capitalist free market will cease to be available; anything that does not find a successful commodifiable form will not survive. Further to this, anything that does not pass the test of the free market ought not be mourned because it must automatically be invalid, illegitimate or unworthy as people cannot desire or want it. This, of course, is because the market is not only assumed to be the formal exchange between free and equal individuals, but is also supposed to represent the aggregate of the social will where the market canvasses unmediated desire. Clearly, it will be necessary to return to this issue in due course, but for now we need only recognise that from this perspective where profit becomes the measure of all social activity we can already see that the market is anything but purely formal. Leaving aside for the moment the discussion of the social operations at work within a market that make it genuinely problematic to speak of it as a realm of free and equal exchange it is clear that market liberalism already contains within it a substantialist argument about what is good and what is not. What is good makes a profit and survives; what is bad runs at a loss and should be allowed to wither and die. That everything gains its legitimacy, social value, and capacity to endure only by securing regular and continuing profit in a market of purely private exchange is exactly the sort of single social goal that Hayek equates with totalitarianism. In every aspect of our lives we are becoming captive to the idea that only the private realm can cater for the variety of personal desires and deliver the breadth of public provision. This means that in every aspect of our lives we are driven by the substantial, unifying goal of profit that takes on 'the characteristic *Gleichschaltung* of all minds' (Hayek 2007:171) that Hayek saw as central to totalitarian efforts at social control. As his editor notes, *Gleichschaltung* was a term used by the Nazis to speak of the co-ordination of 'all political, economic, cultural, and even recreational activities' (171), but the exiled members of the Frankfurt School were writing the same about the nascent totalitarianism they perceived in American capitalist culture where all aspects of life were increasingly co-ordinated through the commodity form.

Hayek's charge is that the planning required by collectivism assumes a 'complete ethical code' (101) that doesn't exist. In such a situation, he contends, the state 'ceases to be a piece of utilitarian machinery intended to help individuals in the fullest development of their individual personality and becomes a "moral" institution [...] which imposes on its members its views on all moral questions [...]. In this sense the Nazi [...] state is "moral", while the liberal state is not' (115). This reference to utilitarian machinery is in a chapter devoted to the rule of law and the need for that law to be purely formal, but what Hayek either fails to see, or actively tries to deny, is that the market already contains the substantial moral claims I have referred to above. His purely 'formal' mechanism already assumes that society should serve the individual first; that self should be privileged over other; sameness privileged over difference; that competition is good; and that the single measure of social happiness should be profit. In fact what this argument about the formality of the Law seems to aim at isn't the importance of formality at all, but the naturalisation of inequality and privilege.

In a striking passage he writes: 'any policy aiming directly at a substantive ideal of distributive justice must lead to the destruction of the Rule of Law' (117). This is because, according to Hayek, the rule of law treats everyone the same: 'To give different people the same objective opportunities', he continues, 'is not to give them the same subjective chance. It cannot be denied that the Rule of Law produces economic inequality – all that can be claimed for it is that this inequality is not designed to affect particular people in a particular way' (117). But what Hayek seems to be relying on here is an argument for a formal system that protects both natural equality *and* natural inequality, depending on whichever one suits his purpose. Firstly, the Law should treat everyone equally because humans are fundamentally the same. They are deserving of protection by the law because they are all by nature reasoning creatures. Hayek's argument is that this can only be done formally, i.e. substantial differences cannot be taken into account because people would not be treated the same. However, if we are supposed to be protecting individuals, what makes individuals individual is precisely the inequality of their experience, biography and material conditions. To abstract individuals from the materiality of their lives is to no longer have individuals but some empty template of sameness that seems rather more totalitarian than Hayek would care to admit.

Secondly, when we do consider material conditions it is perfectly correct, according to Hayek, to accept the economic inequality that we find there. The argument is that because the system of private property reflects a natural condition the inequalities it produces are also natural. The Law as it stands has not designed this, but merely facilitates the natural inequality we find among individuals as they go about their lives. This means that when making an argument about how society *ought* to be conceived we assume the naturalness of formal equality, but if we wish to make an argument about society as it is we rely on the naturalness of substantial inequality. Where Hayek takes this argument, though, is also very revealing and is exemplary of the abstraction and doublespeak so crucial to contemporary idiotism. After the argument has been made supporting both formal equality and substantial inequality Hayek explicitly collapses the two by arguing that the conflict between formalism and substantivism 'accounts for the widespread confusion about the concept of "privilege" and its consequent abuse. [...]

to call private property as such, which all can acquire under the same rules, a privilege, because only some succeed in acquiring it, is depriving the word "privilege" of its meaning' (117–8). In this scenario substantial inequality (the fact that some people have private property and some don't) is nothing but the expression of formal equality (everybody has an equal chance). They are one and the same, and the naturalness of either can be used to support the privileging of the private realm.

UNDERMINING COERCIVE POWER

Like Hayek, Friedman argued that 'the great threat to freedom is the concentration of power' (2002:2), which turns government into Frankenstein's monster. I would agree with Friedman here, but what is so troubling about idiotism is that it refuses to countenance the fact that such concentrated power can stem from the economic realm organised under free market principles. The argument put simply is that 'competitive capitalism [...] promotes political freedom because it separates economic power from political power' (9). This happens because one of idiotism's central articles of faith is that competition inherently prevents power being concentrated in only a few hands. This fundamental tenet, of course, is only thinkable if, like Hayek, thinking is abstracted from the operations and dealings of economic agents within a social context – something I will consider in more detail in chapter four. The economic realm is never so divorced from the legal, political, bureaucratic and communicative components of society as to be able to operate in any pure form. This is nonsense, but it is very self-serving nonsense. Friedman continues by asserting: 'Historical evidence speaks with a single voice on the relation between political freedom and a free market' (9). This is because history is not some objective record of everything that happened, but the selection and interpretation of events by people in socially powerful positions like Friedman. What is often not selected by free marketeers is the testimony of those whose lives have been torn apart by the imposition of free market principles. As one of the axioms of idiotism is that economic freedom is the necessary condition for political freedom, it is expected that people need to be 'freed' from traditional ways of living in order to enjoy the true freedoms that come with the establishment of a free market.

Historical support for Friedman's argument against public intervention or collectivist ideals is also taken from the lives of people of 'individual genius' such as Albert Einstein, William

Shakespeare and Florence Nightingale who made great advances through the exercise of 'strongly held minority views' (4). Again, I have no case to make against the inventiveness of the minority. I would, however, challenge any view that seeks to strip the minority from social or collective practice. After all, don't we know more about the 'individual genius' of Florence Nightingale and less about the 'individual genius' of Mary Seacole simply because Florence Nightingale's 'individual genius' sat much more squarely with our conventional thinking on race and class? In fact Friedman's praise for 'individual genius' does little more than uncritically play out the social conventions that produce historical record. 'Individual genius' is nothing without collective memory, but this connection to the social is precisely what idiotism wishes to deny.

This is not to say that Friedman has no sense for interdependence. Having inherited the work of Adam Smith he is well aware of the need for co-ordination amongst individuals and their families, and like Smith he believes that the free market is the best method for doing that. Like Hayek, it is not that there is no social realm, it is rather that starting from the level of the social or collective can only result in coercion. The market alone stands for voluntary co-operation as it takes as its point of departure the free individual. Friedman writes: 'By removing the organization of economic activity from the control of political authority, the market eliminates this source of coercive power' (15). *This* source of coercive power, maybe, but not every source of coercive power. The problem is that for Friedman *only* political power is understood to be coercive because coercion is something that can only come from the executive function of the state. Like Hayek, however, Friedman can only be this optimistic for free market economics and have such a limited sense of coercion because he has such an abstract and formal understanding of how the market works. Take for example Friedman's idealised description of a free market, or *'free private enterprise exchange economy'* (13). In its simplest form, he writes:

> such a society consists of a number of independent households – a collection of Robinson Crusoes, as it were. Each household uses the resources it controls to produce goods and services that it exchanges for goods and services produced by other households, on terms mutually acceptable to the two parties to the bargain. It is thereby enabled to satisfy its wants indirectly by producing goods and services for others, rather than directly by producing goods for its own immediate use. [...] *Since the household always*

has the alternative of producing directly for itself, it need not enter into any exchange unless it benefits from it. Co-operation is thereby achieved without coercion. (my italics, 13)

This is the simplest form because in actuality the market becomes much more complicated through division of labour and the introduction of specialist enterprises mediated by the exchange of money. But this simplest form of the free market surely assumes everyone has equal access to land and other material resources. How else could each household 'always' have the capacity for direct production should they choose it? How else could each household engage in a 'mutually acceptable' form of exchange, that is in any way meaningful if each household did not have control of the resources that enables the kind of autonomy Friedman assumes to be the case here. What appears incredible to anyone not immediately aligned with this doctrine is that this utopian, if not bucolic Eden of reciprocity and mutuality is taken to be the basis for how exchanges amongst individuals *ought* to take place today. This fanciful vision of some state of nature purity is not in any way hampered by the pristine economics he proposes, it is only undone by politics and the evils of regulation and public intervention. Because his vision is freed from any social contaminant – and this is done simply by refusing to admit that power can enter purely economic relations – his Eden is also free from any and every inequality. Presumably, if a sapphire miner in Madagascar enters into an exchange of his or her labour in return for a pittance, the fact that they would starve if they did not, does not seem to affect the judgement that this remains mutual and voluntary. Coercion does not come from executive diktat alone, but because these exchanges have become so abstracted from real conditions the most obscene inequalities can once again be portrayed as equality.

In Friedman's vision of a free market Eden we can see the spectre that haunts his work. It is the spectre of a bucolic and ancient communism, one where everyone is related on purely equal terms with each having access to the means of production and the free, unalienated access to the results of that production. This is an idealised communism that politics is supposed to have pulled apart and only free market economics can restore, but in many respects this is representative of the uncontaminated worldview essential to every authoritarian movement. It is the purity of such a vision that has given legitimacy to innumerable fundamentalist purges and all kinds of totalitarian violence. What Naomi Klein has called

Friedman's 'rapturous imaginings' (2007:51) certainly permitted the breaking of a lot of eggs when he was given the chance under Pinochet's dictatorship in Chile to rebuild the world in his image. By wiping the slate clean and starting again – Ground Zero for the Chilean population was dated 11 September 1973 – he lived out the revolutionary appeal that concludes Hayek's *Road to Serfdom*: 'If we are to build a better world, we must have the courage to make a new start' (2007:237). However, Friedman's close association with dictatorship brought this call much closer to the kind of 'New Order' (237) politics that Hayek tried to distance himself from. It is just a shame that Hayek did not heed his own warning about best intentions because it was his own vision of flawless economics that set in motion the close association between tyranny and the free market that defines Friedman's legacy.

INITIATIVE AND VIRTUE

I will have reason to return to Milton Friedman in the following two chapters, but now that we have reached the point of ideological rapture it is worth fully embracing this zeal by turning to the work of Ayn Rand. Given that amongst her disciples we can count such once luminary figures as Alan Greenspan, the Chairman of the Federal Reserve who oversaw the economic conditions that led to the 2008 financial crisis, her work is very important from the perspective of the history of ideas. That Rand is a philosophical guru for the free market movement is evident from the phrase that has become the founding axiom of idiotism; Margaret Thatcher's declaration in 1987 that there is no such thing as society, only individuals and their families. This soundbite, as it became, was taken from a comment made by Thatcher in an interview for *Woman's Own* magazine. Along with a couple of other slogans, this phrase came to define Thatcher's revolution and yet its origin lies in the writings of Ayn Rand. In *The Virtue of Selfishness* Rand declares 'there is no such entity as "society", since society is only a number of individual men' (1964:15). In Thatcher's version this is then supplemented by Friedman's argument that the family is the 'ultimate operative unit' (2002:33) in a capitalist system. Together this gives us a very clear indication of the kind of reading material that underpinned Thatcher's privileging of the private both as the realm of the possessive individual and the sector most suited to service delivery. And while Rand might remain something of a maverick for reasons that should become clear, it remains the thrust of Rand's deeply atomistic vision that drove Thatcher's animosity to all things social.

Rand's maverick status is partly due to the fact that she was a novelist by trade, and could not be said to be a professional philosopher or economist. Her non-academic status might give some account of the fact that she does not regularly appear in commentaries on free market economics or libertarian philosophy, but this lamentable by-product of the academy's marginalisation of independent scholars does not give sufficient account for her absence. A more understandable reason is Rand's predilection for taking the rhetoric of the free market and the possessive individual to its logical conclusions, ultimately arriving at something quite unpalatable. But, like pornography, the unpalatable nature of Rand's message doesn't prevent her from becoming an acquired and presumably intoxicating taste in exclusive circles of like-minded people. After all, what ideological free marketeer and tax burdened corporate mogul would not like to hear that rather than being exploitative and greedy they are in fact part of a 'small, exploited, denounced, defenceless minority' (1967:41). This claim from Rand's 1961 essay 'America's Persecuted Minority: Big Business' likens the anti-trust laws in the US to 'legalized lynching' and is the foundation for Greenspan's own distaste for anti-monopoly legislation. The fact that she continues her lament for the poor corporate oligarch by stating that 'every ugly, brutal aspect of injustice toward racial or religious minorities is being practiced toward businessmen' (41) gives some sense as to why publicly embracing Rand's thinking can be problematic. And although there is not room here to set out her various arguments against all things public, her vitriol is most clearly at work in the 1963 essay 'Collectivized Ethics' in which she claims that altruism has undermined the advance of civilisation and has preserved a 'wildlife sanctuary, ruled by the mores of prehistorical savagery' (96). Any glimmer of individual rights disappear as soon as people turn to public issues, she continues: 'what [then] leaps into the political arena is a caveman who can't conceive of any reason why the tribe may not bash in the skull of any individual it desires' (96). The essay then closes with the wonderful rhetorical question: 'Would you advocate cutting out a living man's eye and giving it to a blind man, so as to "equalize" them? No? Then don't struggle any further with questions about "public projects" in a free society' (99). For a system of thought supposedly based in objectivity and rationalism such absurdity is undermining. However, given that to embrace Ayn Rand's thought is to accept the counter-factual argument that altruism is evil, perhaps the idea that America's businessmen are persecuted like no other, or that a sense for social responsibility is nothing more than a desire to dismember disabled passers-by, does not require such an imaginative leap.

Rand's argument against altruism is the fundamental tenet of her thought and clearly sets out the radical, if not extreme, nature of the atomism she propounded. Not only is altruism understood to be evil, but, countering the tradition of utilitarianism that gave rise to free market philosophy, any collective justification for the free market is in turn evil as it assumes altruism or the happiness of others as the basis of one's actions. Altruism is evil, for Rand, quite simply because it '*permits no concept* of a self-respecting, self-supporting man' (1964:ix). Altruism turns individuals towards others when '*concern with his own interests* is the essence of a moral existence' (x). Because, according to Rand, altruism states that any action taken for the benefit of others is good, the only criterion becomes the beneficiary, ultimately leaving man 'without moral guidance' (viii) as to the content of his actions. In the collection of essays entitled *Capitalism: The Unknown Ideal* – a collection to which Alan Greenspan contributed – she writes: 'The *moral* justification of capitalism does not lie in the altruist claim that it represents the best way to achieve "the common good". [...] The moral justification of capitalism lies in the fact that it is the only system consonant with man's rational nature, that it protects man's survival *qua* man, and that its ruling principle is: justice' (1967:12). To understand what Rand means by justice here it will be necessary to work through the system of thought she called Objectivism in order to establish the importance of self-interest, rationality, man's nature, survival and life, and the role of private property in her overall worldview. This will involve a somewhat lengthy engagement justified, I think, by her importance in the pantheon of free marketeers, and because her philosophy carries with it some of the fundamental assumptions and prejudices that will need to be returned to a number of times in the following two chapters.

The opening essay in the earlier collection *The Virtue of Selfishness* is entitled 'The Objectivist Ethics', which restates the claim that ethics is a science. While such a claim is best understood as another symptom of the intellectual fantasy that sought out the philosopher's stone, the claim that human behaviour is reducible to a measurable, quantifiable science is an essential part of contemporary idiotism. Idiotism loves to count. While the status of science in Rand's work is not exactly clear – it is something more than the original meaning of a field of knowledge without ever quite passing the test of being falsifiable – science is used because her ethics are said to be based in a rational description of man's life: 'The standard value of the Objectivist Ethics [...] is *man's life*, or: that which is required for man's survival *qua* man' (1964:25). Science here means the study of '*objective* necessity' (14) as opposed to the study of subjective whim that she claimed dominated the study of the ethics contemporary to her. However, given that her selection of what is necessary for survival seems quite arbitrary it is hard to see how this escapes subjectivism, but that is not the point. What is important is that Rand's Objectivism aims, she argues, to escape the mystical and neo-mystical belief that a system of ethics stems from the supernatural and unaccountable belief in the 'will of God' or its secular counterpart – but equally supernatural – the 'good of society' (15). Indeed it seeks to counter any ethical argument that does not start and finish with the self and its interests.

The argument for the morality of self-interest follows a series of steps. Rand starts with the basic premise that a value is something one aims 'to gain and/or keep' and it 'presupposes an entity capable of acting to achieve a goal in the face of an alternative' (16). Only something alive can face an alternative, therefore only 'a living entity can have goals or can originate them' (16). This means that an organism's life becomes 'its *standard of value*: that which furthers its life is the *good*, that which threatens it is the *evil*' (17). In other words, it is only life that makes value possible, which means the 'fact that a living entity *is*, determines what it *ought* to do' (18). Admitting that the maintenance of life does not differentiate man from other sentient and non-sentient forms of life, she then proceeds to make an argument for what she deems 'proper' to the life of man as his standard of value starting from the most simple awareness of good and evil in the sensations of pleasure and pain. This consciousness of what is good or ill for life is the basic means of survival. For the lower organisms such direction through sensation is automatic and instinctual. The fact that Rand refers to such automatic behaviour as a 'code of values' is something I cannot comment on here, but it does indicate the great leaps in argument that Rand makes without ever seriously setting out how instinctual behaviour can be called a value beyond the simple conflation of life and value. However, man, she argues, has no such automatic code that determines his survival. 'Man's particular distinction from all other living species is the fact that *his* consciousness is *volitional*' (21). Aside from bypassing the a priori condition of being-in-the-world, and assuming an independent subject with the ability to accept or deny the world they are born into, this willful decision making, or the capacity to choose is also conflated with reason. But what is interesting here – although Rand does not seem to consider this might apply to her own thought – is that volition and reason introduce fallibility, which in turn generates the need for responsibility. In other words, 'man has to initiate [thought]. To sustain it and to bear responsibility for its results' (23). In a sense this talk of initiative and responsibility to some extent draws comparisons with Heidegger's argument regarding 'authenticity' and the 'ownmost', but it completely lacks Heidegger's understanding of facticity as being-with-others in a world that necessarily frames whatever decision and initiative we take. When defining such activity she evokes the egoism of Max Stirner who praised what he called 'ownness [as] the creator of everything', the genius that is 'always originality' (1993:163). Her version is to propose that 'everything [man] needs or desires has to be learned, discovered and produced by *him* – by his own choice, by his own effort, by his own mind' (1964:23).

For this claim to make any sense at all Rand would have to be talking about Man as a species, but she isn't, she is talking about individual men. Or, rather, she is talking about both, but this opens up a fundamental fault line that runs through all her work. What is very revealing here is the slippage from the collective use of Man as a species to the use of man as a particular human being. It only makes sense, however, if we refer to this capacity for invention as a collective process, but Rand wants to say that it is individual. Throughout her writing Rand uses the collective noun to define what is proper for an individual, and while it is perfectly legitimate to move from a definition of the human condition to the implications that condition has for each person, what Rand continually aims to do is to extricate the individual and separate it out from any notion of the collective. In the book on capitalism, for example, she writes: 'Men can cooperate in the discovery of new knowledge, but such cooperation requires the independent exercise of his rational faculty by every individual scientist' (1967:7). In other words she perpetually uses the collective and the social as a device for privileging the separate and the individual but never properly argues the case for the move she makes. The same argument appears when she attempts to claim there is no such thing as a 'social surplus' (5). The collective thus remains the unacknowledged ground of her thought, while reason becomes this strange phenomenon, a shared but empty capacity that each individual person fills up with his own concepts.

In this regard she likens human consciousness to a machine brought to life by the will as 'the spark plug, the self-starter and the driver' (23). We might ask how the will can exist prior to consciousness, and we might ask how this can be done without deeming some forms of individual consciousness less willful and therefore less worthy than others, but more immediately how does this explain language, or those concepts we share, or are taught through processes of socialisation that produce a world for us and permit communication? Such solipsism would not permit the kinds of co-operation that even her extreme version of the free market requires. How could such separated, self-starting consciousnesses ever exchange anything when all their time would be spent seeking the means for translating their own worlds into the worlds of others. Again, Rand attempts to reduce everything down to the self-contained, self-generating individual, but all the while deploying some denied element of collectivity to make the whole thing work. In many respects, despite the absurdity of Rand's position, she becomes emblematic of the prejudice that guides free market thinking and the condition I am calling idiotism. It is the unacknowledged presence of the collective as the necessary ground of human relations, or better the active denial of social dependency. In the end, in its flight from the social, this particular version of idiotism forces itself into the contradiction of a communicating solipsism.

What is most disturbing, however, is the way in which this entirely spurious conception of original and productive reason that is supposedly essential to Man's/man's survival is used as a means for devaluing the vast majority of social interaction that operates through liturgy, mimesis, repetition, and adaptation, which is the primary ecology of public communication. Without any account of how communication works Rand dismisses habitual, everyday exchanges in favour of communication that breaks with convention, but any social exchange, indeed any market, *laissez faire* or barter, needs a great deal of ritualistic or confirmatory communication (Carey 1989) in order to function. Where would the New York Stock Exchange be without its bell? There are, of course, great inventions in every social realm. Stock markets have seen their own share of the mathematical wizardry that supposedly changed the nature of risk management, but such innovations would be nothing without the myriad, multiple and rather dull acts of communication that house such invention and permit the particular institution to operate.

A stock market operating at the entropic level of communication
Rand celebrates would be in perpetual crisis. The repetitive and
habitual in our every dealings with others act as the cement within
any formation of human relations, but these are, for Rand, a sign
of lamentable moral failing.

In a passage that reveals the profoundly authoritarian and
dictatorial nature of her work she dismisses the vast majority of
people with the following pronouncement:

> If some men do not choose to think, but survive by imitating and
> repeating, like trained animals, the routine of sounds and motions
> they learned from others, never making an effort to understand
> their own work, it still remains true that their survival is made
> possible only by those who did choose to think and to discover the
> motions they are repeating. The survival of such mental parasites
> depends on blind chance; their unfocussed minds are unable to
> know *whom* to imitate, *whose* motions it is safe to follow. (25)

This passage is extraordinary for a number of reasons. First of all it
is disturbing for its summary production of life stripped of political
protection. In this argument in favour of survival, which is also a
philosophy that supposedly pits itself against the logic of sacrifice
deemed central to altruism, Rand is willing to abandon as parasitic
and subhuman the vast majority of the population who don't
operate according to her own definitions of proper human conduct:
those who don't think or work productively: i.e. initiate. Secondly,
this passage is extraordinary because it raises the Roman principle
of the *res nullius* to the level of thought. This concept of 'empty
space', or unowned space was developed by seventeenth-century
thinkers such as William Petty and John Locke to support colonial
expansion and to justify enclosure of 'empty' or unproductive land.
What is important here is not simply the claim that property is
created through the mixing of labour, but the argument in section
40 of Locke's *Second Treatise of Government* which states that
labour 'put[s] the difference of value on everything' (1952:24). For
Locke, a particular type of labour adds value to the land that would
otherwise go to waste. In line with this, the consciousness of those
Rand describes as 'mental parasites' is equally empty, unproductive
and without worth.

Thus far some sense has been given of what is right, according
to Rand, in the descriptive sense, i.e. a proper description of what
corresponds to Man's true nature as a reasoning, volitional and

ultimately self-starting organism, but it has yet to be shown why the capitalist system is right in the moral sense. To do this it needs to be shown how the standard that is the affirmation of life breaks down into the three values of Reason, Purpose, and Self-Esteem, and the corresponding three virtues of Rationality, Productiveness, and Pride (27). For Rand, a value is something one aims for and a virtue is the means by which one goes about securing it. Immediately, however, we return to the circumscription of key words that permits only one reading of particularly polysemic terms, and to Rand's wonderfully Orwellian double speak. The value of reason is pursued, she argues, via the virtue of rationality, which 'means a commitment to the fullest perception of reality within one's power and to the constant, active expansion of one's perception [...]. It means a commitment to the reality of one's own existence, i.e. to the principle that [...] one must never place any value or consideration whatsoever above one's perception of reality' (28). I say: the sun goes round the earth. Nothing in my experience tells me otherwise. To know the truth I need what Katherine Hayles and others have called the 'extended' or 'distributed cognition' of society. I am unable to find out the truth for myself, but I can find out from others. Of course, Rand would advocate this. It is suggested in the first part of her definition of rationality. But in keeping with her rhetorical style, she immediately wants to privatise this extended cognition upon which we are all dependent. It always comes back to me as ultimate arbiter, as is the case when we morally adjudicate who we should help or who we should condemn: society, she claims, 'has no rights at all in the matter' (93). Despite the caveat about expanding one's perception this is not a dialogical, but a monological model. In fact, this is hardly a recipe for intellectual openness, but for dogma.

It is not dissimilar with the virtues of Productiveness and Pride. Productiveness is defined with a Cartesian bias as the means by which 'man's mind sustains his life' (29). It is not 'the unfocussed performance of some job. It means the consciously chosen pursuit of a productive career, in any line a rational endeavour' (29). It is the path to man's 'unlimited achievement' and represents 'his dedication to the goal of reshaping the earth in the image of his values' (29). If this 'man' refers to the human species then Nietzsche has already told us that human knowledge is nothing but the creation of the world in our own image, but if this refers to men, or individual humans, which it undoubtedly is supposed to, then this can only be tyrannical. Most disturbing, however, is that in a similar fashion to her dismissal of everyday repetitive or ritualistic communication, this vision of productiveness directly excludes a vast number of people whose work within a capitalist system does not permit them any autonomy, let alone the licence to re-shape the earth! If we add to this the definition of pride as the requirement to 'earn the right to hold oneself as one's own highest value by achieving one's own moral perfection' (29), a picture emerges of a thinker who would judge the majority of the population to be 'parasites, moochers, looters, brutes and thugs' (36). And, of course, *one must never fail to pronounce moral judgement*' (82) on such people!

This vision of collectivity as primitive and animalistic brings us back to the question of formal rights. Rand's argument for the primacy of rational self-interest as the basis for morality means that her rights are individualistic in a very specific way. The liberal tradition out of which rights emerged evidently centred the question of right on the autonomous individual, but much of the liberal tradition contains an altruist principle that recognises all people are not equally advantaged and that the state and civil society ought to work towards the enfranchisement of the disadvantaged. To this effect the United Nations charter on Human Rights explicitly sets out what all individuals should have access to in order to safeguard their dignity as human beings. Against this Rand argues 'there is only one fundamental right [...]: a man's right to his own life' (110). Life, of course is reduced to the productivist model of rational self-interest. 'Without property rights, no other rights are possible. Since man has to sustain his life by his own effort, the man who has no right to the product of his effort has no means to sustain his life' (110). The right to property, however, is the right 'to an action' and not 'the right *to an object*' (110). Of course it is a right to an object, but what Rand means here is that there is no right to property or to land, to the means of production or the material conditions that will permit you to live, only the right to get it, and once you've got it, the right to use it without intervention from the state. 'There is no such thing as a right to a job – there is only the right of free trade [...]. There is no "right to a home", only the right to free trade [...]' (114). The reason why we do not need to worry ourselves about the capacity of others to secure the means to survive and be happy is because if they are not operating according to Rand's specific limitations on the right way to live they are ultimately undeserving of any support. This formal understanding of rights is self-fulfilling because anyone with property must be rationally self-interested and therefore deserving, while those without property must be lacking the three virtues – must be an animal, primitive or criminal – and are therefore quite legitimately *undeserving*. The only right, then, is the right to securely use the property gained in the pursuit of rational self-interest; and in this the trader becomes the exemplary figure of morality. Among such men of rigorous moral fibre there is no disagreement because each recognises in the other the necessity of acting to secure the property necessary for life, and each respects the others actions in setting out to ensure they have enough to survive. Objectivist ethics consequently holds that:

> *human* good does not require human sacrifices and cannot be achieved by the sacrifice of anyone to anyone [altruism]. It holds that the *rational* interests of men do not clash – that there is no conflict of interests among men who do not desire the unearned, [...] who deal with one another as *traders*, giving value for value.
>
> The principle of *trade* is the only rational ethical principle for all human relationships, personal and social, private and public, spiritual and material. It is the principle of *justice*. (1964:34)

Over the page she continues to extol traders as people who treat men as independent equals and 'do not switch to others the burden of [their] failures' (35). Today one would have to add, of course, unless they are bankers!

THE STRUCTURE OF IDEOLOGY

While these brief interpretations of Smith, Hayek, Friedman and Rand give some sense of the content of idiotism as an ideology, Rand's definition of Man's productiveness in terms of 'reshaping the earth in the image of his values' gives us the means to discuss the structure of ideology by returning to the work of Althusser. The key here, as noted in the previous chapter, is the role of the image. Although Althusser's specular approach to ideology is better known for adapting Lacan's work on the mirror phase it is his discussion of the specular relation in Ludwig Feuerbach's writing on Christianity where the structure of ideology is most clearly set out. While the mirror function or specular relation is essential to the promotion of specific (partial) views of the world it is also central to the production of any world as such. In the essay 'On Feuerbach' Althusser works though Feuerbach's central claim, as expressed in *The Essence of Christianity*, that 'the object to which a subject *essentially and necessarily* relates is nothing but the subject's *own* essence, but *objectified*' (in Althusser 2003:94–5). In an analysis that prefigures the later philosophy of Husserl and especially Heidegger's writing on the character of Dasein's relation to its world, Althusser shows how Feuerbach developed a theory of the world as a centre constituted by a subject 'from which there emanates a space of objects concentric to this centre, objects objectifying the essence of this subject or being' (95). This circle of objects becomes the subject's horizon. This is a specular relation in which the subject is perfectly mirrored in its horizon of objects. In fact, according to Althusser, the equation allows one to '*approach from either end, subject or object; the result is the same*' (96). Indeed one could start from any one of the specular objects and arrive at the subject. Feuerbach's point, however, was that along this horizon and amongst these objects religion had a privileged position in giving us access to the essence of man. For idiotism this privileged object is, of course, the market.

For Althusser, Feuerbach's specular interpretation of the relation between subject and object gives us a model for the structure of 'every ideological discourse' (99), even if it remains rather naïve. This naïvety stems from Feuerbach's understanding of a correspondence between subject and object where one is recognised in and by the other. To escape this naïvety Althusser deploys Lacan's insight that the specular relation is actually asymmetrical based on a process of misrecognition where an infant's identification derives from the assumption of a specular image (*imago*) of another person that 'anticipates in a mirage the maturation of his power' (1977a:2). The introjected image of the other becomes the basis for future subjective development. In Rand's work the *imago* would be the productive, initiating Subject that is the specular template for every rational and thereby moral being. In keeping with Feuerbach's treatment Lacan also writes that the 'function of the *imago* [...] is to establish a relation between the organism and its reality – or, as they say, between the *Innenwelt* and the *Umwelt*' (4).

The asymmetry is introduced by Althusser through four moves within Feuerbach's model. First, the structure of ideology is 'a specular reflection of correspondence' between subject and object: 'All ideology is essentially *speculary*' (2003:128). Second, the 'speculary structure appears *centred* on the subject' (128). Thirdly, this structure of centring is a '*reduplication*' whereby 'the object of the subject, is also inevitably the subject of the subject. [...] That is why the object of the man-subject is God, who is the Supreme subject' (128). Fourth, and finally, this reduplication is also a displacement of the centring structure on to the reduplicated Subject: 'The relation subject = object [...] takes on a new form, becoming a relation of the *absolute subordination of the first subject to the Second Subject*' (130). As Althusser notes, through this asymmetry the second Subject is sovereign, judge and guarantee, precisely the position of the market and its 'invisible hand' in the ideology of idiotism. For Althusser the 'couple submission/guarantee [...] thus reveals itself to be basic to the structure of any ideology' (130).

To complete this analysis, though, it is necessary to introduce one further element of asymmetry to account for the zealous evangelism of free marketeers like Friedman and Rand and explain why, despite numerous crises and failures, free market ideologues never see capitalism as at fault. This is because the Subject can only remain the guarantor if the specular relation can account for its failure. In this regard, Slavoj Žižek's analysis of desire works especially well. If we take the Subject to be the entity posited to act as guarantor for the world we have created, Žižek (2005) points out that such a guarantor cannot be seen as omnipotent for this would in fact prevent our identifying with it. Instead the guarantor is shown to be lacking in some small degree, just enough to require some supplementary action on our behalf, or for us to find our place alongside it. Just as the evil in the world is not the fault of the Christian God, but our fault for not being sufficiently Christian, so the Market is not to blame for the faults of capitalism. It is our fault for not being economically liberal enough – for not matching up to its purity. This is a complaint regularly found in the writings of the free marketeers discussed above (Hayek 2007:205; Rand 1967:25 and 45; and Friedman 2002:50) who consistently argued that economic crises are not the fault of capitalism – for which we must read the free market – but the fault of governments for not permitting the pure form of capitalism to fully bloom. These zealous disciples see themselves as the correlate of that which is lacking (Žižek 2005:31): the necessary supplement. Their word is the missing piece in the jigsaw and their proselytizing work will bring about an age of fullness, satisfaction and plenitude in comparison to which the present will always be deficient. From such a perspective even when the market is shown to fail *it* did not fail. It was simply let down by those non-believers who do not witness the faith.

Here there is a scapegoat function reminiscent of the need to reaffirm the known world in order to ward off the anxiety brought on by the threat of dissolution. For Heidegger when our world is threatened we either ignore the momentary loss of meaning by throwing ourselves back into practices we know, or, if the threat persists, we become predatory and attack whatever is deemed to be the cause of that threat. In this understanding of both our being-in-the-world and the workings of ideology the system only fails because we are not doing what the Subject wants us to do. Crisis thereby generates more of the same, or perhaps even an increase in the intensity of what we were doing before. While this is a problem integral to any ideology, and one that makes for highly dogmatic practice, it is evident from the work of Hayek, Friedman and Rand that the content of idiotism as an ideology, including elements that are persecutory and authoritarian (if not totalitarian) makes it especially susceptible to the worst consequences of this specular structure. In the next three chapters these basic axioms of idiotism will be considered in relation to contemporary practices in the realms of economics, politics and culture.

3
Idiotism and Economics

By the time the long postwar boom turned into a stuttering and faltering bust in the 1970s the ideology of idiotism was well positioned to present itself as the creed for economic salvation and capitalist resurrection. Or rather, it was argued the time was right for the supposed pure form of free-market capitalism to finally be allowed to operate without public constraint. It was claimed this would deliver the abundance that capitalism had always promised, but due to the interference of governments was unable to achieve. The received picture is that as a result of the neoliberal revolution the last 30 years has been a period of sustained growth, general beneficence and individual freedom only interrupted by the collapse of the financial system in 2007–8, which we are supposed to believe was a catastrophic but unforeseeable accident in a world full of risk. For many, the financialisation of the economy had brought with it an end to the business cycle of boom and bust. In the years immediately prior to the Great Financial Crisis significant figures such as Ben Bernanke, now Chairman of the Federal Reserve, were speaking of the 'Great Moderation' where deregulation, new financial tools and more efficient markets were showing themselves to be the panacea that neoliberals had always claimed, and that capitalism had now begun its path to permanent growth and stability. We no longer needed to worry. The rich had been getting richer, creating a class of such comparative wealth not seen since the days of the European absolute monarchs, but it was claimed that this new aristocracy was fully justified as it steered all members of the global economy to ever greater material well-being.

The fact that there has been a stagnation in growth and a decline in the share of wages as a percentage of GDP in the US from the 1970s to the present (Bellamy and Magdoff 2009:129–30) was regularly denied, as was the condition of millions of newly disenfranchised and landless poor in the developing world. Nor were the free market ideologues concerned by arguments that the financialisation of the economy was in reality only a sticking plaster over the innate tendency of mature capitalism to stagnate and that in the end this revolution that claimed so much would also find itself washed up. Of course, despite the great failure idiotism remains strong. We are so ideologically wedded to privatisation and the free market, and so materially in hock to the financial sector that we cannot properly respond to the financial crisis without proposing something even more revolutionary than the changes that directly led to the system's near collapse. In 80 years, then, we have moved from one depression to another, the latter only being alleviated by some of the lessons learned after the crash of 1929, and a massive injection of public money. As Paul Krugman notes, the restoration of faith in free markets after the crash, on the basis that we supposedly knew what to do in the event of the next crash, was dubbed the 'neo-classical synthesis' by Paul Samuelson in 1950, although Krugman himself prefers the term 'Keynesian compact' (2008:102). However, given the dogma of the free market was seen as a response to the supposed failings of the compact that lifted us out of the doldrums in the 1930s only to deliver the bust of the 1970s, the ghost of Keynes must not be allowed to rear its ugly head for long. Intervention should only be seen as an emergency and therefore temporary therapy for a capitalism that still awaits its own freedom. For the most hardened of the market dogmatists the problem still remains government intervention, and we will only reach the utopia they promise once every trace of government has been removed from economics. And so on we go, with deficit reductions, public sector cuts, and new rounds of privatisation.

Before turning attention to the nature of the revolution that took place from the 1980s and remains dominant despite the Great Financial Crisis it is worth saying something in broad terms about the nature of the business cycle and the proposed solution. This is because it isn't simply a matter of getting the right model of capitalism, but a problem with capitalism itself and its seemingly endless need for expansion. We know that we live on a finite planet with finite resources – finite because there is a limited stock of them, or where they are potentially sustainable our level of consumption outstrips their capacity for renewal – but capital demands constant and compound growth. This is just one of the more obvious but very urgent phenomena that commentators such as David Harvey (1999, 2010) would refer to as a 'limit' to capital. It will be necessary to return to that particular limit below, but to begin to understand how the financialisation of the economy came about we need to revisit the crash of 1929 and the tendency within capitalist systems for overproduction – or the production of a surplus that constantly lacks sufficient places to go in its search for more surplus – with the inevitable result of potentially systemic and hence catastrophic devaluation.

FORDISM TO POST-FORDISM

While the twentieth century was punctuated by numerous business cycles ending in recessions and crises of varying scales, from the 1907 banking panic to the bail out of the giant hedge fund Long Term Capital Management in 1998, followed by the collapse of the dotcom bubble in 2000, it can also be understood as spanning three epochs in the history of capitalism from the age of inter-state rivalry over imperial expansion that resulted in the First World War and the Great Depression; the period of Keynesian economics, the New Deal and the stabilisation of Fordism that emerged out of the devastated Europe that followed; and the global free market that was set to work as the solution for the mixed economy that ran aground in the 1970s. While each of these major periods of crisis, the 1930s, 1970s, and the first decade of the twenty-first century have causes specific to them they can all be understood as manifestations of an underlying problem in the process of capital accumulation itself. As the economy matures its surplus product finds it increasingly hard to find new ways to reproduce itself, either running out of resources, or markets, or running up against a saturation in opportunities to develop the capitalist infrastructure. In 1929 the most proximate causes of the Stock Market crash were political and economic. According to Liaquat Ahamed's brilliant account in *Lords of Finance* the culprits were first of all the politicians who oversaw the peace after the First World War and burdened nations with unsustainable debts, and secondly the central bankers who decided to re-establish the gold standard at a time when very few of the leading economies could cope with the exchange rates that were consequently established (2010:501–2). However, while both these decisions were to some extent correctable, or if they had been made differently some of the problems might have been mitigated, a less proximate yet more inevitable cause for the problems can be understood in terms of overproduction as an internal limit to capitalism's growth.

This problem is primarily found in Marxist and neo-Marxist economics, although a similar problem has received a great deal of attention in more mainstream research where it is associated with the 'stagnation thesis' of the American Keynesian, Alvin Hansen.

As Bellamy and Magdoff put it: 'Hansen focused on the specific historical forces that had propelled the capitalist economy [...]. As *historical* forces these were transitory and waned over time' (2009:13). In addition to this, as has been mentioned already, the maturing of the capitalist economy meant that traditional investment opportunities were drying up as investment 'became increasingly geared to mere replacement [...] with little new net investment' (13), which all meant that capitalism had to seek out new historical forces or development factors that would enable it to grow. Looking back over the twentieth century, with its regular cycles of boom and bust it is not hard to see how this problem lurks beneath all the explanations of the most proximate causes, but it is one that many economists would rather not address precisely because it suggests a problem with the fundamental axioms of the capitalist system as a regime of accumulation rather than a problem pertaining to levels of regulation and methods of management. However, the most compelling argument in favour of the stagnation thesis is Milton Friedman's claim from within the midst of the postwar boom that the theory 'has been thoroughly discredited' (2002:76). The problem, of course, as will be shown in more detail below, is that positivism does not possess anything that even closely resembles an historical sense and can thereby easily confuse historical factors for universal truths.

In an excellent study of the birth of consumer culture Martyn Lee (1993) sets out the historical factors that led to the 1929 crash as well as the stabilisation of Fordism that followed, and it is this analysis that is the key to understanding the full flowering of the consumer culture and the credit boom of the 1980s which in turn led to the Great Financial Crisis of 2008. Following the Marxist approach outlined above Lee understands the overproduction problem in specifically technological terms. The emergence of the innovative methods of mass production that we ordinarily associate with the first automated Ford factory in 1913 potentially opened up new avenues for investment and new means for accumulation. Together with the introduction of Frederick W. Taylor's methods of organisation as set out in his *Principles of Scientific Management* of 1911, a new path to greater productivity and hence greater profits was developed as production became both faster and more efficient. However, other historical factors were to not only hinder this new regime of accumulation, but would ultimately lead to a system-wide crisis. As Lee (1993) points out:

a regime of accumulation should be able to secure the long-term quantitative and qualitative supply of labour-power commensurate with the scale and form of the prevailing mode of production. It should be able to guarantee a labour market of a sufficient size and possessing the appropriate skills that are needed for the given mode of production. In other words, it must be able to stabilize wage or labour relations. Second, a regime of accumulation must also be able to guarantee the appropriate market capacity needed to match both the quantitative and qualitative nature of the commodities being produced. It must ensure a large degree of compatibility between the spheres of production and consumption, between the production of use-values and the scale and consumption of needs. This is the requirement to stabilise commodity or exchange relations. (76–7)

He then goes on to say that a problem with labour relations leads to a crisis of production while a problem with exchange relations leads to a crisis of consumption, and by the late 1920s production in the US was drifting inexorably towards both.

The introduction of scientific management techniques was accompanied by a new wave of labour disputes where workers refused to be reduced to the level of the 'trained gorilla' that Taylor suggested would make 'a more efficient pig-iron handler' (in Gramsci 1971:302), but it was the problems with exchange relations that are most important for the argument that follows. For Lee, the problem here was that the emergence of mass production heralded the creation of the *intensive* phase of capitalist accumulation while the system as a whole was still geared to the *extensive* phase associated with the imperial, nation-state phase of capitalist accumulation. Here the historical factors enabling growth were the colonial expansion into new markets, new resources, and new pools of exploitable labour. In keeping with this, what Lee refers to as 'competitive regulation' (77) ensured the low wages, and hence low labour costs that best suited this extensive mode of accumulation. However, as Lee puts it, a significant problem arose when it became evident that 'geographical expansion alone could not sustain indefinitely the current rates of productivity. In order to remain viable, the productive apparatus would soon need to consider a radical form of vertical expansion within its market potential if the dynamic nature of the new productive system was not to outstrip the limits of demand' (77).

Coupled with the unworkable levels of debt that a number of countries were saddled with, plus the premature return to the gold standard, this period of transition where capitalism required a consumer culture that wasn't yet established meant that the system ran into the perfect economic storm and collapsed under the pressure. The depression of the 1930s brought about a sea change in thinking about the economy. Having been dominated by the non-interventionist policy of the free market, economics began to move away from the classical vision of economic freedom and move towards an acceptance that the state may be required to act beyond its juridical-militarist role and become directly engaged in economic matters. While Henry Ford himself tried to stimulate the market by raising wages, a phenomenon that Gramsci saw as 'an objective necessity of modern industry when it has reached a certain stage of development' (1971:311), the state was soon to follow with the implementation of Roosevelt's New Deal between 1933 and 1936; a series of state programmes designed to inject massive investments into a system that needed emergency resuscitation. 1936 was also the year that John Maynard Keynes published *The General Theory of Employment, Interest and Money* that crystallised the new approach and became the cornerstone of the welfarism that shaped the development of advanced capitalist economies over the next 40 years.

For Keynes, capitalism was simply too unstable for the market to be left to its own devices. And while it took Hansen to draw out the full implications of Keynes's thinking regarding the tendency towards stagnation, Keynes himself realised there were inherent flaws in the capitalist mode of accumulation, especially relating to the need to find investment opportunities for the surplus it produces, shortfalls that, as Bellamy and Magdoff explain, could emerge from an 'overcapacity in plant and equipment, a sense that the market for consumer goods is or will soon be saturated, a perception that the external frontier for expansion is limited.' (2009:13). All three of these can be seen to have caused investment problems for the early Fordist mode of production, for without the requisite demand it soon reached overcapacity and soon experienced a saturation in the market, while the waning of the first extensive phase of capitalism also brought it up against the limitation of the external frontier. But there is one other factor at work here that Keynes spoke about in *General Theory*, and this is what he called 'animal spirits'. The problem for investment is that it is always based on some future projection, but such projection is always uncertain given the internal limits that can always scupper predictions. Added to this, though, is the fact that investments are also based on *feelings* about the future and not just rational calculations. This means that capitalist investment is risky and unpredictable because of unforeseeable formations in its internal limits *as well as* potentially bipolar emotional responses ranging from euphoria to depression in our anticipation of what lies ahead. This, then, is indicative of another fundamental limit. Emotion and affect are central to the speculative moment in all capitalist investment, and Ahamed paints a vivid picture of the role they played in the meltdown of 1929 in the wake of stock market hysteria (2010:343–4). Successive booms and busts would also readily map onto a chart of affective fluctuations in the psychology of investors and consumers. 'Animal spirits' is such an important phrase that George A. Akerlof and Robert J. Shiller claim that 'just as Adam Smith's invisible hand is the keynote of classical economics, Keynes' animal spirits are the keynote to [...] a view that explains the underlying instabilities of capitalism' (2009:xxiii).

Of course, it requires no leap of the imagination to see that the very idea of an invisible hand is nothing but an expression of animal spirits, representing our desire to posit order or our will to believe in some benign entity reflecting back and confirming the supposed perfection of our own creations – the very structure of ideology set out in the previous chapter. However, it was Roosevelt's New Deal and Keynesian economics rather than the market that steered capitalism out of its crisis via what came to be known as the mixed economy; a putative third way between planned and market economies. While the planned aspect of the mixed economy carried with it certain socialist traits that included the idea of state intervention and a heightened role for public services, the intervention on behalf of the state was also profoundly capitalist in that the state was a key agent in the development of the early consumer culture. In line with the sociological component of Fordism, in which the Ford Motor Company actively engaged in a biopolitical programme aimed at shaping the behaviour and home life of its employees, the new state-capital matrix set about developing the necessary agencies to ensure that 'the mass of ordinary people [...] both think and behave in a manner which is broadly supportive of the prevailing economic and political interest' (Lee 1993:86). Without such co-ordination between the needs of capital and the desires of the populace, capitalism would quickly run up against its limits. The household and domestic relations were therefore absolutely crucial here as traditional forms of domestic production such as dress-making and baking, for example, had to make way for the consumption of prefabricated commodities. Given the gender relations of the time women were established as the carriers of the new ideology and were educated in the correct forms of consumption, which eventually included the extension of Taylorism into the home. By the 1960s the kitchen had become the centre of consumer efficiency, in which new appliances testified to one's participation in the modern age, and the ubiquitous use of plastic evoked the alchemy of 'infinite transformation' (Barthes 1973:104) that would become the defining feature of consumer culture's maturity.

From the 1930s through to the end of the 1970s the welfarism of the mixed economy became the largely established wisdom where government oversight and intervention could make up for any unforeseeable risks that might cause a downturn. Public spending became the new means for quickly exiting a recession and re-establishing growth. In this model large public programmes would take up any slack in private investment. The theory of the mixed economy also benefitted from the three key features that Bellamy and Magdoff argue are essential counters to stagnation. First of all, the age of post-colonialism gave birth to new nations. This was also the first stirring of a neo-imperialism of both the capitalist and communist variety as each side sought to bring the emerging nations and the respective labour pools within the influence of their own mode of production. Secondly, there was the Second World War, in which state spending on the military initially pulled economies out of the depression, while postwar reconstruction, supplemented by the Marshall Plan, ushered in the boom of the 1950s and '60s. Thirdly, and of equal importance to these world changing events was the popular adoption of the motor car. Again, as Bellamy and Magdoff point out, the car completely transformed both the US economy and society. While the take up of the personal computer and the related use of a variety of mobile media have provided a focus for recent investment in the 1990s and 2000s, it has never been on the same scale as the motor car. The new digital technologies, despite being economically and socially transformative, were not able to absorb the surplus in the way the motor car did. The point about the car is that it required a massive road building programme, which included bridges and tunnels, not to mention petrol stations (and petrol production), roadside service stations, garages, and spare parts factories. However, when the creation of the suburbs is factored in, a demographic development entirely reliant on the motor car, the scale of social change that resulted from one technological innovation is almost incomparable (2009:41). These opportunities for investment helped placate what David Harvey calls the 'capital surplus absorption problem' (2010:26). However, like all other things these are historical factors and they have a tendency to wane. Eventually, the market for the car met early problems with saturation and competition from abroad, and the welfarism of the mixed economy that had instilled in workers, who had never been in such a strong position under capitalism before, a sense of their own importance as wealth creators and the desire for greater equity in the surplus they produced. The general argument is that an increased round of labour disputes not only upset the delicate balance of wage relations, but also brought about a period of inflation as capitalists tried to recoup the losses in labour costs by raising prices. This was accompanied by an inability in the mature formation of Fordist production methods to respond to innovations in production coming from overseas; the so-called 'Japanisation' of the factory that would later constitute capitalism's reformation along flexible, post-Fordist principles. Not only, then, did the capitalist mode of production need to re-imagine itself in line with new automatic and communicative technologies that would permit much greater responsiveness to ever growing, but ever fragmenting – that is, de-massifying – markets, it also had to maintain exchange relations in keeping with the maturing and globalising consumer culture. This time, the answer to the sclerosis that seemed to have gripped advanced capitalist countries was believed to lay in sweeping privatisation, the freeing up of industry from the red tape of regulation, and the release of under-used capital reserves to greatly extend credit. Enter Margaret Thatcher.

DEREGULATION AND FINANCIALISATION

On assuming office in 1979 Thatcher embarked on a radical privatisation process that included selling off British Telecom, British Airways, British Rail (including both the physical infrastructure and the licences to run services), the utility companies, the national coal industry (which was also the height of her sustained attack on organised labour), and council or public housing. In terms of the financialisation of the economy, one of the first things she did in 1979 was to immediately abolish exchange controls, thereby opening the UK up to the free flow of an ever-globalising capital, and in a successful bid in 1986 to prevent the City losing its status as the world's financial hub her government enacted a process known as the 'Big Bang' in which a range of alterations to financial regulations repositioned London as the world's leading financial centre. Coupled with the promotion of a consumer culture fuelled by cheap credit she oversaw a decade in which any residual pre-war virtues such as thrift were replaced by greed and excess. The amount of money flowing into London in particular saw massive infrastructural developments and a housing bubble that inaugurated large-scale gentrification (plus the social cleansing that goes with it) of numerous London boroughs.

However, the idea that privatisation produces a profit for the public purse is highly debatable. As John Quiggin points out, privatisation 'will yield net fiscal benefits to governments only if the price for which the asset is sold exceeds its value in continued public ownership. This value depends on the flow of future earnings that the asset can be expected to generate' (2010:185). The method for assessing this is complex and controversial not least because of what is known as the 'equity premium puzzle'. Put very simply the equity premium is the difference in the return from bonds and stocks (equity) with stocks on average giving a 6 per cent higher return than bonds (Quiggin 2010:189), something explained by the fact that stocks are much riskier and therefore generate a higher return. For privatisation, however, this is a problem because a government can fund expenditure solely through the issuance of bonds whereas investors buying public assets will be investing as if they were buying stocks. In the numerous instances of privatisation that Quiggin studied he found that most cases resulted in a net loss for governments, aside from sales that had gone through in bubble conditions. He picks out Thatcher's sale of British Telecom as an especially good example of this bad trade.

Consequently, if the equity premium puzzle casts doubt over the benefit of privatisation for the public purse we have to assume that the benefits lie elsewhere, namely, in the role the principle of 'accumulation by dispossession' (Harvey 2003) has for private interests and more generally for capitalist expansion. The *idios* as private enclosure has been the primary means for capitalist accumulation over the centuries, and while in the developed countries this has significant effect on the shaping of services, in the developing countries where the majority of people still depend on the commons, dispossession of such resources can be absolutely devastating. Privatisation is often advanced through the use of debt as a stick with which to beat developing countries into submitting to the free market via the imposition of the enclosures or 'structural adjustments' demanded by the IMF in exchange for bail outs. Accumulation by dispossession therefore takes many forms. The primitive form of land and resource privatisation is still of major importance, while in the more developed countries it is the stripping of socially owned industries and services. However, as Harvey notes, new forms of accumulation by dispossession include patents and licencing on genetic material; intellectual property rights; biopiracy; and the commodification of cultural creativity (2003:48). In light of this the putative benefits of privatisation for the public purse are ultimately an irrelevance. Dispossession by enclosure, or the shifting of resources from the public to the private, both of which are signalled in the use of the term idiotism, are essential to the advancement of capital. Firstly, social or public ownership is a blockage to the free flow of capital, these are resources upon which capital cannot feed or invest its surplus. Secondly, dispossession, especially in the developing world produces a pool of landless labourers separated from traditional forms of production and now dependent upon capital for survival (with the additional benefit a putting downward pressure on wage demands).

Privatisation was thus one arm of the doctrine known as Thatcherism that responded to the over-accumulation problem that resurfaced in the 1970s. The second arm of the response was the financialisation of the economy that benefitted from the deregulation integral to privatisation. In the United States, just as in the UK, there was a raft of legislation aimed at deregulating financial markets culminating in the 1999 abolition of the Glass-Steagall Act, which had been passed in 1935 to set up a firewall between retail and investment banking in the wake of the 1929 crash. In a move that shows just how little has changed since the 2008 crisis the 'radical' proposal of *introducing* a firewall (it is presented as something *novel* rather than simply putting back what should never have been removed) has now been shelved in the UK until 2015. The end of Glass-Steagall was preceded by the Garn-St. Germain Depository Act of 1982 allowing savings and loans companies to expand into new businesses, an act that Johnson and Kwak note was hailed by Reagan as the 'first step' to 'comprehensive deregulation' (2010:72). The Secondary Mortgage Market Enhancement Act of 1984 then allowed investment banks to buy up mortgages, pool them together, slice them up and resell the repackaged slices in a process known as securitisation. That was followed by the Tax Reform Act of 1984 that created tax incentives for investment in securities, and if there was one innovation that can account for the economic and political rise of the financial sector it is securitisation. This process of slicing and dicing mortgages and re-selling the bundle allowed banks to mix elements of high risk loans with medium and low risk loans, thereby spreading and supposedly lessening the volatility of investment because the instability of high risk is now set off against the low risk securitised in the new bundle.

Unfortunately, there isn't room here for a full analysis of the crisis in 2008, but there are a number of very good accounts, the best of which, at least in terms of the most proximate causes, are John Lanchester's *Whoops!* and Johnson and Kwak's *13 Bankers*. The point to make here, though, is the complicated relationship to risk that the financial sector developed. It would not be right to say that securitisation was productive because it got rid of risk; the point is that it enabled banks and other financial institutions to expose themselves to higher risks and higher yields. This was possible because they believed a tool had been created that would prevent exposure to high risk taking them down because their exposure to it was spread. As Lanchester notes, 'the world of money is all about risk: seeking it, and seeking to master it' (2010:123). From government bonds to personal mortgages the equation is simple, the higher the risk the higher the yield. The task was to find a way to make high-yield, risky loans that brought in ever greater profits while minimising critical exposure. With the creation of securitisation the financial sector, increasingly 'liberated' from any oversight, believed it could pursue ever increasing risk with ever decreasing concern.

It should be added that securitisation also allowed the bundles to be sold to other investors meaning that risk was passed from lenders to others further along the chain, which may have included banks, hedge funds and an array of other financial institutions. Given that securitisation had shifted the risk from the lenders to investors, lenders 'now had no need to be particularly bothered about whether or not the borrower could repay' (Lanchester 2010:99). This opened up the sub-prime lending that would eventually bring the system to its knees. Believing that risk had been sufficiently dispersed the industry took on greater exposure to high risk thinking its distribution throughout the system was diluting it. However, the quantity of high risk taken on in the pursuit of huge profits ultimately meant that the entire system became contaminated. In effect, lenders were given the green light to lend money to anyone irrespective of the ability to pay, all under the misguided premise that, with house prices continuing to rise, everyone would eventually benefit. Added to this was the blinkered attitude whereby 'in an era of free market capitalism triumphant, an industry that was making so much money had to be good, and people who were making so much money had to know what they were talking about. Money and ideology were mutually reinforcing' (Johnson and Kwak 2010:6). Ultimately, what was created was a giant Ponzi scheme in which the lenders had no other remit than getting more people involved. Once the poor people who could never repay the loans they were sold defaulted, and because there were now so many of them, the contamination brought down the entire system. That was until it was bailed out with public money. In Lanchester's words securitisation ended up magnifying the risks: 'It's as if people used the invention of seatbelts as an opportunity to take up drunk-driving' (65).

The attractiveness of securities such as Collateralized Debt Obligations, insured by the newly invented Credit Default Swaps (for an excellent account of this see Johnson and Kwak 2010:121–6), was enhanced by the AAA rating given to them by the rating agencies. These agencies, the big three being Standard and Poor's, Moody's, and Fitch, deserve a great deal of attention because they epitomise the dogmatically closed system I am calling idiotism. However, due to constraints of space I will limit myself to a key few points. In the first place it should be noted just how important their incompetence was in the crisis of 2008. It was these agencies that rated the new financial tools AAA. This is equivalent to saying they were as safe as the very safest investment, namely US government bonds. Not only does this show how flawed ratings can be, and how catastrophic a flawed rating is, but it hides the fact that the inventors of the financial tool pay for the rating and they tend to pay the agency that gives the best rating. This is the philosophy of providing the customer with what they want taken to absurd levels. Secondly, these relatively small private firms have established a significant influence over national economies due to their central role in financial markets, especially as the financialisation of the economy has become the dominant regime of capitalist accumulation. Most people should now be aware of the ratings agencies, not least since Standard and Poor's downgraded US bonds in 2011 to AA+. Here we have a private firm effectively dictating economic policy to the world's most powerful nation.

This is understandable from two perspectives set out by Timothy J. Sinclair in his excellent book on the agencies' power. Firstly, while the judgements of rating agencies are ideologically presented as if they were descriptions of a naturally occurring and incontestable phenomenon, ratings are inherently subjective. The agencies thereby need to prevent any 'sudden collapse of their epistemic authority [...] by presenting themselves as strong' (Sinclair 2005:177). Such a challenge to the administration of Barak Obama is certainly a show of strength. According to Sinclair their power stems from political consent. As will be explored in the next chapter, the close ideological ties that now exist between the political class and capitalists means that rating agencies can be used to justify policy changes that are mutually beneficial to a constellation of different political and economic nodes of power – something that in the next chapter will be referred to as a transnational capitalist class. As Sinclair goes on to say, this has great significance for what might be called national policy autonomy. Ratings agencies therefore 'represent the shape of newly emerging authority' (175) whose power is 'camoflauged' (175). This was exemplified in a speech made in October 2009 by the soon to be new British Prime Minister David Cameron in which he declared the budget deficit to be a 'clear and present danger'. Here we have a prospective national leader (of one of the world's biggest economies) using the dramatic language of the sovereign, the language normally used when justifying the declaration of war or a state of emergency. And yet the danger was that Standard and Poor's (again) had threatened to downgrade the UK's credit rating unless the government pursued a programme of deficit reduction, which would automatically include a new round of privatisation. Despite Cameron's posturing as the heroic sovereign what we in fact have is a nation bending its knee to the subjective whim of a small private company. Fundamentally, this is what 'pleasing the markets' means, something Paul Krugman argues encourages governments to make perverse rather than sound policy decisions (2008:113).

My point, however, is that this situation radically undermines the idea of national sovereignty in any meaningful sense. Cameron doing what Standard and Poor's tell him to do is not the action of a sovereign, but a puppet. Ratings agencies therefore epitomise idiotism because they are indicative of how private interests have come to dominate, even subjugate public concerns, but also because they represent the closed nature of the system. This is because in an age of a globalising financial economy it is what Sinclair calls the 'mental framework' of the agencies that has formed the new political consensus:

Based in markets rather than formal government structures, bond rating is at odds with the consensus that underpinned the post-World War II political economy of embedded liberalism. That postwar world order was built on a compromise between producer and consumer, owner and worker, investor and employee. The work of bond rating agencies, as the mental framework of rating orthodoxy suggests, implicitly attacks these compromises and promotes the interests of investors. Rating agencies should be understood therefore as a crucial nerve centre in the world order, as a nexus of neoliberal control. Like an operating system in a personal computer, ratings agencies, although usually unseen, monitor global life at the highest levels, with important social and political effects. (Sinclair 2005:69–70)

In short, the agenda of privatisation most suitable to investors is now rigorously pursued by national governments seeking to 'please markets' under the threat of a downgrade. And nowhere are the political implications of idiotism more starkly presented, for nowhere is public policy so clearly directed by private interests.

The environment in which the rating agencies awarded AAA ratings to CDOs and CDSs was one in which the role of 'quants' or mathematicians had greatly increased. It was now the 'quants', rather than economists or traditional bankers, that were measuring risk and were integral to the industry-wide acceptance of the 'Value at Risk' (VaR) model. VaR became the statistical model accepted by the industry for calculating the probability of deviations in risk which ordinarily appear as the Greek letter Σ, sigma. According to Lanchester, VaR became the accepted model because it worked in *most* cases. However, it also seemed to evaporate risk as can be seen by the 1998 Russian bond default and collapse of LTCM being viewed as a seven-sigma event. 'That means', Lanchester observes, 'it should statistically have happened only once every three billion years' (139). What is extraordinary here is not only the capacity for the chosen statistical model to be wrong, but that the industry was so blinded to systemic risk, and so dogmatically convinced that it had found the holy grail for infinite capital accumulation that they continued to use this model that told them, despite the evidence, that nothing was wrong. By the time the full crisis hit Lanchester recalls that David Viniar, the CEO of Goldman Sachs, was talking about twenty-five sigma events happening every few days, and wryly notes: 'Remember, what we're talking about here is a drop in house prices which caused people with bad credit to have trouble paying their mortgages. That was turned into something that was literally the most unlikely thing to have happened in the history of the universe' (140). The irony of Hayek's complaint regarding pseudo-scientific theory becoming part of socialism's official creed (2007:173) should not be lost on us here!

However, the reason the myth of the Great Moderation held despite the numerous crashes, bail outs and recessions was because those at the top were making a lot of money, but more broadly it was believed that the financialisation of the economy with its emphasis on speculation and credit remained the best means of responding to the problem of over-accumulation and the long slowdown of the 1970s. As the Great Depression of the 1930s showed, part of the problem was a need to develop sufficient demand, and, as Bellamy and Magdoff argue, this is the basic conundrum of capitalism; it is a process of accumulation 'that depends on keeping wages down while ultimately relying on wage-based consumption to support economic growth and investment' (2009:27). It is for this reason that the neo-liberal agenda of Thatcherism that operated in part through the primitive accumulation of privatisation also promoted a consumer culture fuelled by relatively cheap credit. Paying workers more money it was claimed would only further destabilise the economy so capitalism responded by generating huge pools of debt. While debt has a very important regulatory or disciplinary function in that the profligacy that is encouraged immediately becomes a source of power for those issuing the credit, the key feature to be addressed here is the two-fold cure that credit offered. Firstly it gives workers, now fully enfranchised as consumers, the ability to buy more commodities, but the extension of credit is also a way to make money from money. The over-accumulation problem was seemingly diminished by this dual motor for securing and reinvesting surpluses.

Absolutely central to this was the deregulation of financial tools and the banking system, which also involved the rapid development of the shadow banking system, which grew to approximately the same size of the traditional banking system in just over a decade. This shadow system includes non-depository banks, or institutions that borrow and lend money, but are not governed by traditional banking regulations. Such institutions include investment banks, hedge funds, structured investment vehicles, money markets, and insurers, with Lehman Brothers being the most high-profile victim within this sector during the 2007–8 crisis. To be precise, though, as Krugman (2008:163) notes, it is not necessarily deregulation that was the problem, but the fact that this huge sector in the financiali-sation of the economy was completely free from any oversight in the first place. To understand the vulnerability of this expansion in finance it is important to understand that this surfeit of credit was only possible if the cash ratio or reserve requirements of banks were drastically cut. While the reserve has been traditionally seen as a safety cushion in times of crisis, i.e. if there was a panic and a run on the banks they would have some money to pay back depositors and creditors. In 2006 in the US the reserve requirement was cut to 10 per cent. This means that a bank can lend £1,000 pounds to another bank who can in turn lend £900 (keeping £100 pounds in reserve) to another bank who can in turn lend £810, etc. Now while this represents the genius of the banking system in that it can create £2,710 from £1,000 (and of course much more should the lending continue), this also means that £1,710 that is in circulation doesn't actually exist, that is, if everyone asked for the money back at the same time someone would be left carrying a large debt. This is why liquidity is so important because if the debt doesn't keep moving, then, like a shark, it will die. A crisis in confidence causes liquidity problems because people stop lending and the debt stops circulating. The financial crisis was in effect a giant game of musical chairs where more and more chairs were being taken away but no one was bothered because they had forgotten that someone at some point was going to stop the music. While this might seem irresponsible, if we add to this the increasing importance of the shadow banking or non-deposit banking system and the fact that the reserve requirement in this sector (which would include savings accounts) was cut to zero in the US it becomes clear that this was a recipe for disaster.

As far as the financeers or the 'banksters', as Lanchester calls them, were concerned the cash ratio was a waste of a vast reserve of money that should be put to work rather than lay idle, especially because the main area of 'productivity' was no longer the production of consumer goods, but the surplus value taken from the financing itself. Where Marx's classical formulation of the cycle reads $M\text{-}C\text{-}M^1$, where M is money, C is commodities and M^1 is profit, the new regime of accumulation could be formulated in the following way: $M\text{-}M^1$. Money was now making money without needing to be diverted through the costly and complex mediation of commodity production, which in an age of maturing infrastructure and markets was becoming increasingly hard anyway. The importance of finance to the new regime of capitalist accumulation is evident from the fact that almost every major retailer or producer set up its own financial arm as supermarkets launched their own banks and vehicle recovery firms moved into insurance, but it is also starkly set out in two sets of figures. Firstly, Johnson and Kwak show that while financial sector profits grew in line with non-financial sector profits from the 1930s to 1980, 'from 1980 until 2005, financial profits grew by 800 percent [...] while nonfinancial sector profits grew by only 250 percent' (2010:60). If we add to this the fact that 'the ratio of outstanding consumer debt to consumer disposable income has more than doubled over the last three decades from 62 percent in 1975 to 127 percent in 2005' (Bellamy and Magdoff 2009:29) we get a very clear picture of what was happening. This has two implications. The first is that the financialisation of the economy was of less benefit to those dependent upon the 'real' economy and disproportionately benefitted the financiers. It was therefore only a very limited solution to the slowdown of the 1970s. Secondly, it would have been those on lower incomes that would have been saddled with the proportionately greater level of debt. This would have been in part due to the call to be good citizens and consume as much as possible, but it is also the case that low income families use credit as a means of managing the increased risk brought about by the gradual dismantling of the welfare state and the volatility of the new labour conditions (Quiggin 2010:25–7). In the words of Bellamy and Magdoff it was 'class war waged unilaterally from above' (2009:61).

During this period what had been dubbed the Great Moderation was in fact the generation of a series of bubbles in different parts of the globe that permitted a continued, but disseminated speculative frenzy. As Harvey notes, in this mode of accumulation 'the crisis tendencies are not resolved but merely moved around' (2010:117). While Greenspan's creation of a housing bubble as a response to the dotcom crash is the most infamous, this mode of accumulation is really a giant global froth – capiccino, even – where bubbles, both small and large, are perpetually created as financial capital flows around the world. The lack of oversight and regulation that facilitated the financialisation of the economy was in part deemed necessary to set dormant capital to work, but it also emerged in a climate of increasing moral hazard. As Krugman explains, this was a term that first emerged in the insurance industry to describe a 'situation in which one person makes the decision about how much risk to take, while someone else bears the cost if things go badly' (2008:63). What allowed the financial sector to be so lackadaisical about regulating risk was because under this regime of accumulation 'the moral hazard game is played at taxpayers' expense' (64). What became known as the Keynesian compact as a response to the Great Depression gave an increasingly important role to central banks as lenders of last resort. As has already been noted, in this role the function of central banks was to add stability to a system that had been shown to be very fragile. Although the Great Depression stemmed from the crash of 1929 it was the panic of 1907 that eventually brought the Federal Reserve into existence in 1913. While Keynes's interpretation of the business cycle was given further support in the 1970s through the work of Hyman Minsky and his 'financial instability thesis' the slowdown was the opportunity for classical economists to reassert their belief in free markets. While Minsky lost the intellectual battle over deregulation, at the time the central banks remained lenders of last resort and throughout the period of free market resurgence played an important part in responding to the various crises that erupted. The financial crisis in 1987 saw Alan Greenspan inject liquidity into the system, an action that became known as the 'Greenspan put', named after a put option that guarantees the price of an asset, and by the time the Fed bailed out the hedge fund Long Term Capital Management in 1998 (Krugman 2008:134–8) the financial sector came to believe that the Fed could and would bail them out of any crisis. As a staunch free marketeer Greenspan was opposed to a central bank interfering in bubbles, which would have been the Keynesian approach, and focused instead on the recovery. So by the end of Greenspan's tenure the role of the central bank had shifted from prevention of crises to the guarantor of any wager a financial institution wished to make. The state in the shape of the central bank acting as the underwriter for casino capitalism is another key feature of idiotism. Defenders of the free market would, of course, still blame the crisis on the public institution for encouraging such moral hazard, but one could easily blame it on the blind faith in markets to regulate themselves and therefore not require such intervention.

RATIONAL MARKETS

Of central importance here was something called the Efficient Market Hypothesis (EMH), which John Quiggin (2010) includes in his account of the ideas that should be dead but somehow still seem to be walking about. In brief it is a theory claiming that markets are the opposite of the casinos that the Great Financial

Crisis showed them to be. As Quiggin explains, the hypothesis 'says that financial markets are the best possible guide to the value of economic assets and therefore to decisions about investment and production. This requires not only that financial markets make the most efficient possible use of information, but that they are sufficiently well-developed to encompass all economically relevant sources of risk' (2010:35). It also required the market to be as liquid as possible in that all markets should be brought into the global free market ensuring the free flow of capital, which in turn necessitated large rounds of privatisation in numerous countries, especially those with socialised economies. The thinking behind EMH is also the theory that gave us the market in terror mentioned in chapter 1 and was popularised, as Quiggin notes, by books such as Thomas Friedman's *The Lexus and the Olive Tree* that told governments 'they could not possibly hope to resist the collective financial wisdom embodied in the "Electronic Herd"' (42). The thesis assumes, then, that the stock market and asset markets necessarily offer the best estimate of the right price of stock. This price emerges out of a complex set of relations and actions that make it impossible to anticipate the market as the so-called 'chartist' (market predictor) assumed. The thesis is most closely associated with the work of Eugene Fama in 1970, but can be said to have started with the innovative work of the French statistician, Louis Bachelier, whose theory of the 'random walk' in 1900 countered the idea that future prices could be predicted. In seeking to predict, the market investors were looking for market inefficiencies or moments when the market got the price wrong. Prediction, however, could only work on past prices, but the possibility that prices could go on a random walk caused by some as yet unaccounted for event, plus the idea that knowledge of any inefficiency would soon become public and prices would consequently adjust, meant that the market was practically always right and couldn't be beaten.

Johnson and Kwak explain that EMH comes in three versions: the weak version stating that future prices can't be predicted; the semi-strong version, that prices adjust quickly to all available information; and the strong version, where no one has information that can be used to predict prices, therefore prices are always right, and by right, this of course means that they bear some relation to underlying, real economic values. They go on to say, that despite some 'caveats' expressed by Fama, 'the strong form became the intellectual justification for financial deregulation. If a free market will always produce fundamentally correct asset prices, then the financial sector can be left to its own devices' (69). What is more, as Quiggin notes, once EMH becomes the orthodoxy, that is, it is accepted by economists and politicians alike 'there is no need [for governments] to worry about imbalances in savings and consumption' (2010:49). What is interesting about this argument is not just the idea that the market is always and necessarily right, which is a central feature of idiotism as it is to be understood in relation to economics, but that a theory derived from work positing the primary nature of the unpredictable should become so satisfied that it had adequately factored in all the determining elements that allow markets to be taken as self-organising stabilizers when it clearly hadn't. According to Johnson and Kwak the general, and erroneous, economic principle is that 'given perfectly rational actors with perfect information and no externalities, all transactions should be beneficial' (69) because they are always based on the 'right' price. The fact that the collapse and public bailout of Long Term Capital Management in 1998, and the bursting of the dotcom bubble in 2000 categorically demonstrated that markets don't get the price right seemed to have passed by supporters of EMH. What is even more remarkable is that the crisis of 2008 has done little to dent the common sense faith in markets.

Although EMH was challenged by numerous economists, in fact, according to Johnson and Kwak, relatively few believed the 'assumptions actually held in the real world' (69), it nevertheless came to dominate public policy alongside another theory of complex processes known as Dynamic Stochastic General Equilibrium (DSGE), which also privileged the rationality of actors and the efficiency of markets. For the purposes of the argument in this chapter and the setting out of idiotism as it pertains to economics I will limit myself to a few points from the very broad arguments that have taken place over a number of decades about the nature of macroeconomics. With the crisis in Keynesian economics in the 1970s the opportunity came to revisit classical economics with its privileging of individual utility. From the 1930s onwards the orthodox view had been that public or state intervention was needed to dampen the worst effects of market instability and that the state needed to intervene in areas of production, consumption and labour relations in order to manage and thereby lessen any damaging imbalances. However, for economists like Friedman the approach where government expenditure made up for a decline in private expenditure was deeply flawed. As he famously remarked: 'Unfortunately, the balance wheel is unbalanced' (2002:76).

According to Friedman, because government expenditure only had effects after the end of the recession it was intended to intervene in, such a blunt instrument simply contributed to inflation, a higher tax burden, and further government intervention. As such, intervention was 'itself a major form of disturbance and instability' (77). The key, or so it was believed, was to return to the natural regulators of the free market, namely self-interest and the maximisation of utility that founded classical economics. In other words come up with a macroeconomics based in classical or neoclassical microeconomics. From this emerged the monetarist approach, presented in the book Friedman wrote with Anna Jacobson Schwartz (1971), in which government intervention was limited to the control of the money supply via short-term modifications in interest rates.

To get back to the DSGE model, it is the tinkering with the monetary supply that explains the dynamic stochastic element, where dynamic in economics represents the temporal component and stochastic refers to the element of chance or risk. Government or central bank control over interest rates should allow for the management of both unexpected upturns and downturns as they appear over time. However, all of this is possible because the economy is made up of rational, utility maximising agents. The theory of general equilibrium assumes the equilibrium of supply, demand and prices across a set or even the totality of markets, and can model this by aggregating the behaviour of economic agents. It is understood to be a general theory because it expands on the theory of partial equilibrium used to analyse specific markets. The general theory assumes quite logically that the condition of one market is necessarily related to conditions in other markets, and that the interrelationship produces its own equilibrium. However, the reason why the theory can assume equilibrium and suggest the image of a gently stirring body of water, is because it assumes all agents, be they individuals or firms, to be rational, and it is this rationality that enabled market liberals to wish away the tidal wave that hit the shores of the financial sector in 2008.

The theory is said to have originated with Leon Walras in the 1870s, and was later developed in the 1950s by Kenneth Arrow and Gerard Debreu, to which was added the theory of 'rational expectations' in what became known as the New Classical school. According to the strongest version of rational expectations, which the New Classical school adopted, it 'required all participants in an economy to have, in their minds, a complete and accurate model of that economy' (Quiggin 2010:93). A major influence was Robert

Barro's work in 1974 that, as Quiggin notes, drew on the classical economics of David Ricardo. For Ricardo, if a government goes to war all citizens should anticipate a rise in taxes. As Quiggin observes, according to this theory rational citizens would save 'by an amount equal to the additional government debt' (94). This assumption of rationality does two things. Firstly, 'in competitive markets where participants are perfectly rational and display high levels of foresight, it is very hard to see any beneficial role for governments' (Quiggin 2010:106), given that this rationality has a tendency to produce equilibrium. Secondly, should this equilibrium not be achieved it is merely the fault of irrational individuals whose behaviour removes any justification for state assistance. It was no accident that the first government to adopt the thinking of the New Classical School was the Thatcher government in the UK. Her indifference to the disequilibrium that followed in the wake of her economic revolution was in part due to her own inability to empathise, but it was also implicit in an economic theory that was fundamentally sociopathic.

The rethinking of macroeconomics from the perspective of classical microeconomics is important for understanding idiotism because it assumes the primacy of the individual, but it also does so by de-emphasising the influence of public institutions or wider social factors. Absolutely central to this component of market liberalism, then, is the conception of the individual, and by extension the definition of human nature summed up by the tenets of rational choice theory, a useful analysis of which can be found in George DeMartino's *Global Economy, Global Justice*. The three fundamental propositions of this theory are the 'consumption proposition'; the 'production proposition'; and the 'scarcity proposition'. Paraphrasing DeMartino the consumption proposition states that 'individuals are endowed with the ability to choose rationally from among the set of opportunities' they are confronted by, with rationality signalling that individuals will decide according to the opportunity affording the greatest satisfaction or utility. This includes a secondary assumption of 'insatiability', meaning that we always prefer more satisfaction or utility rather than less. The production proposition claims that 'humans are endowed with the ability to transform elements of nature (through work or labour) so as to produce goods that meet human needs, and they do so rationally', while the scarcity proposition states that all output (in form of goods and services) requires inputs from nature and since nature's bounty is finite, output must also be finite. Economics thus becomes the study of rational choice under conditions of insatiability and scarcity (DeMartino 2000:38–41).

What is important here is that this not only produces the perfect model for a rationally competitive equilibrium, but it also assumes an individual whose choices are exogenous, that is, both external and prior to social activity and influence. The individual is therefore very much modelled on the interiority of the *idios* in which every expression of desire or need is based on a radically personal calculation of utility. While the production proposition contains a notion of rationality that carries with it Locke's philosophy set out in chapter 2 that justified the enclosure of common land, the production proposition is therefore a further justification for the supposed efficiencies of privatisation over the inefficiencies of public works. That said what remains most extraordinary about DSGE is that because its account of rationality is assumed to be universal it is a model that works with only *one representative agent* (Quiggin 2010:108). One of the greatest ironies, therefore, is that a model which is central to a philosophy purporting to be the best means of guaranteeing individual liberty has a conception of individuals as interchangeable units operating according to an automatism reminiscent of the most dystopic collectivisms. Modelling DSGE needs only assume the actions of one agent because every agent is the same. For Quiggin, the dogmatic nature of this approach to the economy was revealed in a comment made by David Gruen, who worked for the Australian Treasury in the run-up to the financial crisis and likened the neoclassical macroeconomists to people on the *Titanic* who had locked themselves away 'in a windowless cabin, perfecting the design of ship hulls ... for a world without icebergs' (in Quiggin 2010:82).

The iceberg hit in 2008 because the models of efficiency and equilibrium precisely failed to take into account the social factors involved in economic relations. In the first instance the economic account of efficiency was based upon an entirely inadequate account of information and communication that assumed both sufficiency and transparency. Johnson and Kwak do point out that with regard to EMH the economists Brad DeLong, Andrei Schleifer, Larry Summers and Robert Waldmann had in fact come up with a model 'showing that "noise trading can lead to a large divergence between market prices and fundamental values" [and] that it was impossible to differentiate between noise and information' (2010:69–70). Here, the concept of noise will have been taken from Claude Shannon's 1948 article, and later book of the same name, 'A Mathematical

Theory of Communication', which was highly influential in the burgeoning field of cybernetics and related systems theory, where a noise source was placed between the information source and the destination to stand in for the possible barriers to successful communication. As a mathematician working in an engineering laboratory Shannon was especially interested in technical barriers to effective communication, but also suggested the possibility of 'semantic noise'. While there is an argument suggesting that Shannon had little interest in 'meaning' (Liu 2011), humanities disciplines such as cultural studies have made much of this idea of semantic noise in a culture containing actors who may operate within very divergent fields of experience, or what Wilbur Schramm called frames of reference (1971:31). Such fields introduce the idea of encoders and decoders of communication (24) who will not necessarily be communicating with the same code as they don't live/ operate within the same frame of reference. In societies as culturally complex as those in advanced capitalist countries the opportunities for noise disturbing the efficient exchange of information is potentially dramatic.

This leads to a second major problem with theories of rational efficiency and equilibrium, namely the evidence that clearly demonstrates people do not always and sometimes only rarely act in accordance with the maximisation of economic utility. As was noted in the early part of this chapter, one of Keynes's greatest contributions to economics was the recognition that 'animal spirits' are absolutely essential to the movement of the economy. For Akerlof and Shiller animal spirits are 'a restless and inconsistent element in the economy', referring 'to our peculiar relationship to ambiguity and uncertainty' (2009:4).

Animal spirits are indeed profound, but paying 'attention to the thought patterns that animate people's ideas and feelings' (1) is really only the start of the matter. The centrality of emotion rather than calculation to the capitalist system is plain to see in the word for the mechanism that was once the oil that merely lubricated the motor, but has now become the motor itself, namely credit. The root of the word is the Latin *Credo*, which means belief. This belief is printed on our bank notes, which are nothing more than promissory notes, committing someone at some point to exchange it for the equivalent in gold. However, as long as the money circulates, as was noted earlier, and as long as I can pass on the promise to someone else in exchange for a good, then I don't need to go to the Bank of England and redeem it for gold. This then introduces the other absolutely essential belief, made to be fair on the basis of probability, and therefore on a calculation of risk, that not everyone will seek to redeem the notes for gold at the same time. Improbable or not, there remains a strong element of belief, or to use another favourite phrase of economists and business pundits, confidence. The point simply is that the capitalist system, despite claims to rationality, remains a belief system. Not only that, its complexity necessitates a great deal of trust. Confidence or trust is rational for economists, but as Akerlof and Shiller note 'the very meaning of trust is that we go beyond the rational. Indeed a truly trusting person often discounts or discards certain information' (12). The importance, but also the instability of trust is brought into a sharper focus by Geoffrey Hosking who, in his beautiful little book on the subject, writes: 'Trust is crucial because it is the tool we use to face our own future' (2010:3). We know the future has a certain quotidian regularity, but it is also highly and radically unpredictable. If trust, itself extremely fragile, is the tool we use to face up to it, it immediately becomes clear how delicate and resistant to rational calculation our lives are. The presence of emotion or feeling is also in evidence when we consider other social relations where 'consideration of fairness can override rational economic motivation' (Akerloff and Shiller 2009:22). It is often the case that people make decisions based on moral or ethical principles that directly counter their immediate self-interest. We could, of course, re-embed moral judgements back into a wider conception of utility where agents imagine an immoral world as one they would not be happy in, but the making of moral decisions by agents in a complex economy is very hard to predict, given that the conception of justice is itself incredibly slippery.

Returning to the question of prices that the EMH assumed were always right, Akerlof and Shiller point out that prices are often dependent not on information but on guess work about what other people think (133). Future prediction of stock prices, for example, is not necessarily based on hard and fast facts about a company's performance and knowledge of changes in the economy, but on guessing how others might feel about the value of that stock. Golden Delicious apples are everywhere, they claim, only because people see them everywhere and assume that everyone likes them (134). It's a self-perpetuating fallacy. What else could explain the ubiquity of this rather tasteless fruit? There is, then, a strong feedback between price and animal spirits, they argue, and this feedback is notoriously difficult to predict. As Krugman notes, the qualitative fact of feedback is not the problem, but 'its quantitative strength' is (2008:91). At times where the quantitative strength is high and negative, this can produce a profound loss of confidence and a catastrophic crisis.

Akerlof and Shiller, however, introduce another important element to the complex influences on prices, and this is the existence of stories (2009:51). Because we are not isolated, utility maximising, rationally calculating monads, but the product of a whole complex of social relations – where my thoughts and desires are extended out through others in a myriad of ways only to fold back in to me in ways that make it very hard to lay claim to them as authentically mine – stories are essential for the binding of the collective behaviour we call confidence. Stories, Akerlof and Shiller argue, move markets, but not because they explain the facts, the stories '*are* the facts' (54). Stories of a new era and the Great Moderation boosted confidence, much as the technophilia and euphoria around digital technologies produced the dotcom bubble. Stories are not second order phenomena that explain reality, but are imbricated in the production of reality itself. As was noted in chapter 1, the world is something primarily interpreted and stories are the setting out of this interpretation. It is also important to note here that in Heidegger's analysis of our being-in-the-world interpretation is always already accompanied by something that Akerlof and Shiller might call feelings, but which Heidegger refers to as Dasein's 'mood'. This is the primordial and pre-theoretical way in which we encounter the world. By this Heidegger means that our mood or the manner in which we are 'attuned' to the world is '*prior to* all cognition and volition, and *beyond* their range of disclosure' (1962:175). What is more, he explicitly makes the claim that in 'looking at the world theoretically we have already dimmed it down to the uniformity of what is purely present-at-hand' (177), in other words, viewing the world and the beings of which it is comprised in purely abstract terms as is clearly the case with both the EMH and DSGE's denial of the embedded, embodied and messy relations that make up each and every economy. We are always in some mood or other, then, and there can be no attunement to the world that is moodless. Even the purest of theoretical approaches has its mood; one of detachment, perhaps. This means that stories and the moods that motivate our choice of story, not only enable us to understand the fluctuating and unpredictable states of confidence, they also give us access to the pre-theoretical and un-conscious aspects of our being-in-the-world that radically undermine idiotism's claims about the bounded, rational individuals upon which the entire edifice of neoliberal dogma depends.

For Akerlof and Shiller, then, it is human psychology that drives the economy, and the story of the dotcom bubble affords the perfect opportunity to consider this claim about the role of the unconscious and the irrational in relation to market efficiency. The dotcom bubble happened because of stories about the impact of digital technologies and the internet. Stories circulated not only about the take up of the personal computer and the popularity of surfing the web based on empirical evidence derived from the market, these stories drew upon an older, and often told story about the utopian possibilities of technology. Such a story is regularly juxtaposed by the technophobia of Frankenstein's monster, which at the time was creating problems for another emerging technology, that of genetically modified food. However, these competing stories are in turn the manifestation of an even more archaic narrative about future destruction or salvation. While GM food suffered from Mary Shelley's take on the apocalyptic narrative, digital technologies rode high on the spirit of messianism that is ordinarily reserved for a religious context. Of course, investment in digital companies was based in pragmatic economic decisions about the opportunities new technologies offer for solving the surplus problem, but the idea that these specific technologies might be *it* encouraged an enthusiasm that went beyond the rational – given that many of these companies weren't even reporting a profit – supported by the deeply embedded cultural myths about the future and technology's role in it.

PURE ECONOMICS

This evidence for the role of psychology and the social in the realm of economics also challenges the climate of economic positivism in which the EMH and DSGE were cultivated. While the work of Hayek in the early part of the twentieth century might have seemed radical, if not heterodox, the argument for a realm of pure economics had gained ground in the writings of Rand, and more importantly Friedman. As Johnson and Kwak have indicated, there was a growing belief that *political* economy was only for developing countries. In those already developed it was assumed that 'economic questions could be studied without reference to politics', and that economic and financial policy presented only technocratic questions' (2010:55). However, aside from the technocratic issues addressed above there was a genuine belief that a pure capitalism was not only possible, but also necessary. As Friedman put it, 'the great threat to freedom is the concentration of power' (2002:2) but pure market capitalism supposedly escapes this problem because it 'separates economic power from political power' (9). Aside from the fact that this is patently incorrect given that the deregulation needed for a free market requires the law-makers being brought on board, the idea that economic power, i.e. material wealth does not result in political power is absurd.

While free marketeers recognise the political influence and economic danger of monopolies they perversely blame the state for their existence. Although economic history clearly shows a period in which the state, especially the US government, was closely involved with the creation of monopolies this does not mean the state is the only source. While Hayek, for example, regards 'capitalist organizers of monopolies' as a source of danger and speaks of a 'corporative society in which organized industries would appear as semi-independent and self-governing "estates"' (205), he quickly reverts to type claiming this is not actually the fault of capitalists, but the state who help them enlist support from other groups (205). In keeping with this Greenspan argued that monopolies are primarily the product of public policy. Although he conceded that competition is an active and not a passive noun implying 'the necessity of taking action to affect the conditions of the market in one's own favour' (1967:68) he claimed that, in a laissez-faire economy, competition is regulated by the market as regulator of prices (69). Likewise, in an image not dissimilar to that suggested by DSGE, Hayek offered a cybernetic view of the market as a de-centring but self-organising system of information that resists the capacity to co-ordinate and thus assume power over the process (2007:95). All of this though clearly ignores the fact that there is a tendency towards concentration of companies, whether that is in a supposedly 'free' market or in a managed economy. Look at any area of business and the trend towards ever larger transnational corporations is clearly evident. In an important area such as the media this is especially pronounced with only six or seven of the largest companies such as News Corp dominating the vast majority of the world's media. The influence if not control that Rupert Murdoch held over the British Parliament was plainly set out by the *News of the World* scandal, but uncovering the illegal activities of one newspaper owned by a News Corp subsidiary hardly undoes the corrupting influence of big business on democratic life. As Galbraith points out the idea of pure economics and the impersonal market is a fraud.

Everyone knows that the 'free' market is extensively and expensively managed in association with news and entertainment programmes (Galbraith 2009:17) to the benefit of those in power. To deny this in the name of objective economics simply shows how claims to scientific knowledge are socially and politically biased.

Deregulation, then, was the means by which free market ideologues sought to remove the danger of public influence over the economy. According to Greenspan, not only would this ensure the end of monopolies it would have the additional effect of dis-empowering the capitalist in relation to consumers who would receive greater protection without government oversight. In an essay entitled 'The Assault on Integrity', which is worth quoting simply to show just how deluded the chairman of the Federal Reserve was, Greenspan argued that the greed of businessmen was a consumer's best protection (1967a:126) because they will only make money if they retain their reputation, which is thus 'a major competitive tool' (127). Regulation, he goes on to say, 'undermines the moral base of business dealings. [...] A fly-by-night securities operator can quickly meet all the S. E. C. [Securities and Exchange Commission] requirements [...]. In unregulated economy, the operator would need to spend years in reputable dealings before investors would trust to place funds with him' (129). Reputation and virtue are thus capitalism's motivating power (130). What we in fact got after almost three decades of deregulation, privatisation and the promotion of markets was the unbridling of a degenerative greed, and a society almost completely in thrall to the power of two very specific capitalist estates – the financial sector and the military-industrial complex, ably supported by the media. Despite creating a supposedly politics-free economy there has emerged, through what Johnson and Kwak call the 'revolving door' between Wall Street and Washington (2010:92) a financial oligarchy that has taken over policy in the US, with a military wing that secures the global free market by force if necessary, and all the while the media represent this as free, democratic, accountable, open and just. Although the Wall Street–Washington corridor may have become the main conduit for the growth of market dogma, how idiotism has come to flood the *entire* socio-political field needs to be discussed in the next chapter.

4
Idiotism and Politics

There has always been a strong link between the *idios* and the *polis*. From the origins of our concept of democracy in Ancient Greece until the institution of universal suffrage in the twentieth century the ownership of private property has been central to the concept of citizenship and to full participation in political life. This material qualification for public life has also been supplemented by a more existential one whereby the retreat to the private realm, to the peace and quiet (σχολή) of private reflection, has facilitated the productive relationship between philosophy and politics, and provided the necessary space for the recuperation of energies believed essential for the rigours of political office. The use of the private as a *solution* to the problems of public life has also had a long tradition as shown in chapter 2, but it was not until 1989 when the destruction of the Berlin Wall supposedly signalled the death of communism that idiotism came of age. At this time the Western model of a formally democratic liberal capitalism could finally and permanently be held up as the undoubted victor. Communism continued elsewhere, but the only other major player outside the Soviet Union, the People's Republic of China, had already started to open up and introduce the dual track of capitalist economics and communist politics, a system that Rand would more readily describe as fascism (1967:239). China to some extent had already proved the West right, at least economically, but that was all that mattered. Nevertheless, the fall of the Berlin Wall was accompanied by an overture of academic hyperbole best captured in Francis Fukuyama's essay and later book *The End of History and the Last Man*. While he has had to overturn his thesis with the political and cultural rise of Islamism, the emergence of alter-globalisation movements, and the introduction of radical new technologies, the argument has remained part of idiotism's common sense.

To some extent this is surprising given that the overall argument of the book is predicated on an absurdity, but this is the point. It was not so much that history had come to some kind of naturally evolved final state, history was being *declared* over. The book's title was more of a *performative* statement than a descriptive one. It represented the move on so many fronts that announced the end of history, and with this the end of public life as we previously knew it. That the public realm has always had close ties with the ownership of private property has meant that political life has been marked, in the main, by the defence of privilege and the maintenance of the status quo, but due to its fundamentally antagonistic character it has also seen the periodic instituting of profound, if not revolutionary change in answer to the big questions of public life concerning, amongst other things, what it means to be human, and the nature of the Good society. Since 1989, however, such arguments have been declared over. To some extent these questions persist in ethical debates on the use of human tissue, and around genetics and cloning more generally, but these are largely epiphenomenal debates that do not challenge the established doxa regarding human nature and the suitability of a formally democratic capitalism to best serve that nature. Alternatives to capitalism – even alternative models of capitalism such as Keynesianism – had supposedly faded away. With the fall of the Berlin Wall the only political goal left was to fully globalise the free market: to dispense the good news of free market solutions to every part of the world. The free market would become ἡ οἰκουμένη, the whole of the habitable globe. What Fukuyama did get right, however, or at least partially right, was that while the debate concerning the best way to live and organise ourselves had been decided, in practice the future would not see more formally democratic capitalist countries, but a rise instead of authoritarian capitalism (1992:122–4). In many respects this is true. Contrary to the writings of a number of his conservative allies, whether we look at the Chinese system, the mafia capitalism or oligarchy in Russia, or the numerous capitalist despots that supported Bush and Blair in their invasion to liberate, or rather liberalise Iraq, Fukuyama is borne out by this fit between authoritarianism and capitalism. Why he was only partly right, however, is because he failed to see, or perhaps refused to countenance, the possibility that previously liberal capitalist states like the US and the UK would become increasingly authoritarian.

Idiotism as it pertains to politics is precisely this shift from social pluralism to the dogmatic application of privatised solutions, the commodity form and the unitary goal of profit to all aspects of social life. It is a matter of both ideology and of organisation, both of which I will consider here. In some areas of academic debate, this dual process has come to be known as depoliticisation. At one level this registers the move from politics understood as an agonisitic concern for public issues to a putative consensus around the privatised model of consumer choice, where the major concern is which school to send little Johnny to. But depoliticisation is a constellation of related processes, one of which is this ideological claim for a post-political world in which it is argued that the best method for social organisation has now been decided. Linked to this are two other intimately connected features that epitomise the functioning, or organisation of idiotism as a dogma. The first is the emergence of managerialism across every sector of public life. Ordinarily managerialism is associated with the massive bureaucracies of collective or state enterprises, but today we have a form of decentralised, micro-management the task of which is to ensure that every social sector – especially where these are still understood to be public works – adopt the new mantra of profit, customer service, monetised output, competition, and markets in all areas of endeavour. A consistent mantra of idiotism is that decentralisation equates to greater flexibility and freedom when in fact decentralisation is really a more mobile method for the installation of a unitary goal. Each institution might be given the autonomy to run as an individual business, but to do this the managers must instantiate the right thinking within its workforce that will enable the institution to operate according to the unitary goal of profit. Connected to this is the formation of what Leslie Sklair (2000) and others have called a transnational capitalist class (TCC) comprising not only the members of corporate boards, but also politicians, industrialists, regulators, media moguls, managers, military leaders, and high ranking civil servants. Such a class represents the diverse agents required for both the global circulation of discourses and representations that best promote the ideology, as well as the organisation of key social and political institutions responsible for the decisions, techniques and technologies that enable the smooth pursuit of surplus value in all areas. Managerialism is a key disciplinary mechanism that ensures society operates collectively in the interests of the TCC.

DEPOLITICISATION

The dominant view, then, is that the tearing down of the Berlin Wall and the collapse of communism equated to the institution of a consensus around the positive qualities of capitalism and has heralded the arrival of a post-political age. When I speak of depoliticisation, however, I have no intention of suggesting that politics is over, rather that politics is increasingly reduced to the logic of the market, both in terms of ideology and organisation. As Jodi Dean (2009) has pointed out politics on the right remains strong. In the USA especially, numerous areas including education, health, reproduction, gun law and the environment, to name only a few, remain hotly contested areas of political life, and we need only add the previously mentioned alter-globalisation movements and Islamism to get a sense of just how political the times we live in actually are. For some on the left, then, the argument regarding depoliticisation is in fact indicative of a failure of political thinking. Dean, for example, argues that the 'political intensities' we find expressed today in the relatively new phenomenon of digital petitions have become 'shorn of their capacity to raise claims to the universal, persisting simply as intensities, as indications of subjective feeling' (2009:32). In such a situation the left loses its commitment both to activism and a collective project, and practices its politics instead as a series of specific, often private, and not necessarily related moral responses or monetary donations.

For Dean, though, the new medium of the internet is only partly responsible. What is also crucial is that the left has abandoned its commitment to solidarity, and because 'neoliberalism eliminates the symbolic identities made available under Keynesianism', without the left remaking claims to universalism 'identities are too fleeting and unstable to serve as sites of politicization' (73). To what extent the left ought to seek out a universal claim is a contentious issue, which I will reserve for the final chapter. My point here is simply to support Dean in arguing that depoliticisation is a problematic term as it tends to dovetail with the more conservative claims regarding post-politics. For me idiotism is not the evacuation of politics from social relations, nor does it signify a cynical or defeatist resignation to the idea that our current system is the only game in town. Rather, thinking idiotism in relation to the political is to think of the political in the seemingly contradictory process of depoliticisation. Idiotism is the belief that the traditional questions of the *polis* are best answered by the market, and the dominant *political* force is an alliance of interests that establishes procedures for the realisation of this vision.

In relation to the first element of political idiotism, namely the belief that the market can and should replace politics, the work of Milton Friedman is definitive. While his work represents a certain free market extremism, and could therefore be said to be peripheral to some elements of current thinking even within supporters of free market economics, his work most clearly represents idiotism's logic. It is not that Friedman has been refuted, economics is not a science and therefore cannot be subject to refutation in that sense, it is more the case that for his supporters the opportunity for establishing Friedman's utopia has not yet arisen. In *Capitalism and Freedom* Friedman argues that the free market can stand in for many of the activities traditionally covered by politics because the market is in fact a very workable system of proportional representation (2002:23). This claim is something of a double negation of the political. As has already been shown in chapter two, the kind of positive economics that Friedman espoused had already rendered the political irrelevant for the study of economics, which had both a disciplinary and practical purity. Here, however, he recognises what most would refer to as the political, but argues there need not be any political realm other than the market. Certainly if we understand the political as the realm for the expression of desire concerning how people wish to live and how that desire is to be serviced, the market, for Friedman is the ultimate and only gauge.

In keeping with Hayek's criticism of politics directed towards collective goals he argues that the 'widespread use of the market reduces the strain on the social fabric by rendering conformity unnecessary with respect to any activities it encompasses' (24). Although I have also argued in chapter 2 that this hides the unifying social goal of profit, Friedman is adamant that the market equates to pluralism: 'The wider the range of activities covered by the market, the fewer are the issues on which explicitly political decisions are required and hence on which it is necessary to achieve agreement' (24). This is an important topic as it clearly demonstrates that the putatively socio-political pluralism promoted by contemporary idiotism is based solely on the economics of consumer choice. This in turn is determined by the existence or not of commodities to satisfy that choice. Meaning that any social relation, activity, or object that cannot be successfully and consistently commodified does not appear in this market system of proportional representation. In fact it is not represented at all, meaning this is a rather restricted conception of pluralism: only that which can operate through the commodity form can be represented. What is significant here is that this claims to be a model for social and political freedom when the social and the political have already been decided. The questions concerning how we should live, the nature of the social bond, our relations to others, and how that is represented, or directly practiced, have now been concluded in favour of the mediation of the commodity form. Ordinarily such a conclusion to social and political matters, and such a mechanism of social and political organisation would be declared authoritarian, if not totalitarian by these so-called defenders of freedom. It is only the sleight of hand that turns the identical into the plural that permits the word 'market' to exempt itself from such a designation.

In this model of marketised politics the role of the state is reduced to protector, enforcer and umpire in all issues pertaining to the general and formal laws agreed upon to secure the free disposal and exchange of private property. Such formal laws Hayek originally likened to the establishment of the Highway Code that enables free and safe passage for individuals on British roads, rather than specific rules 'ordering people where to go' (2007:113). In Friedman's version of the liberal tradition the state should limit itself to the maintenance of order and the issues of justice that protect a free market, and should adjudicate and arbitrate in matters where 'neighbourhood effects' make strictly voluntary exchange impossible. Here Friedman offers the example of a polluted stream where those who use the stream are forced to 'exchange good water for bad' and aren't able to 'enforce appropriate compensation' (30). To paraphrase, the list of the important functions a government may perform includes the following: the maintenance of law and order; the definition and, where necessary, modification of property rights and rules of the economic game; adjudication of disputes about rules; enforcement of contracts; promotion of competition; provision of monetary framework; prevention of technical monopolies; and the supplementing of private charities and families in protection of the irresponsible, namely the mentally ill and children. Those practices out of bounds for a government include: Import and export tariffs; rent control; minimum wage or maximum price; detailed regulation of industry or banking; control of media communications; social security programmes, especially pensions; licencing; public housing; conscription in peacetime; the postal system; and toll roads (34–6).

However, this rolling back of the state and government functions does not mean that other political issues such as the fight against discrimination are not important to Friedman. Quite the contrary. That Friedman believes the free market to be the ultimate social panacea can be seen in his claim that 'the groups in our society that have the most at stake in the preservation and strengthening of competitive capitalism are those minority groups which can most easily become the object of distrust and enmity of the majority – the Negroes, the Jews, the foreign-born, to mention only the most obvious' (2002:21). Just prior to this Friedman argues that the free market was the best defence against McCarthyism because the existence of a private market economy gave government employees alternative sources of work. If the government controlled and regulated all employment how could those charged by Senator McCarthy have hoped to find work once they had been blacklisted? According to Friedman, 'an impersonal market separates economic activities from political views and protects men from being discriminated against in their economic activities for reasons that are irrelevant to their productivity' (21). The idea that what protects people here is their 'productivity' rather than any civil or political right they might hold is rather chilling and does chime with many dystopic visions of society where one's only protection is the capacity for effective work. In many respects, contemporary immigration laws are moving in this direction, where those seeking asylum and protection within the framework of political liberalism are increasingly vilified as scroungers, while those making a claim for residency based on the principles of economic liberalism – skills, productivity, growth – receive some modicum of protection. One of the least obvious features of idiotism, then, is this privileging of productivity over persecution in our consideration of the needs of non-nationals.

In the chapter entitled 'Capitalism and Discrimination' Friedman goes as far as to argue that the migration of Puritans and Quakers to the New World was possible 'because they could accumulate the funds to do so in the market despite disabilities imposed on them in other aspects of their life' (108). The fact that the New World was discovered with the funding of an absolute monarch is alluded to by Friedman, but quickly passed over. Despite his arguments for pluralism he really doesn't like the complex and messy picture of the network of socio-political conditions that led to the formation and colonisation of the Americas. Likewise when he turns to the America that was contemporary to the writing of his book he is happy to reduce the advancement of black politics in the US to the 'maintenance of the general rules of private property and of capitalism [which] have been a major source of opportunity for Negroes and have permitted them to make greater progress than they otherwise would have made' (109). Reworking the earlier argument about productivity he states that 'there is an economic incentive in a free market to separate economic efficiency from other characteristics of the individual' (109), but I am not aware of any demand emerging out of the civil rights movement that drew attention to a black person's equal capacity for economic efficiency. The intention here, of course, is to bypass any reference to such a political movement and claim progress in social and political matters solely for free market economics. It is self-evident, however, that if all job opportunities were at the whim of the government and the government was racist there would clearly be a problem, but this has never been the case in the US. Add this to the fact that not only racism but the genocide of native Americans was taking place in the US when it was supposedly at its most economically liberal and the suggestion that the free market undermines institutional racism becomes totally absurd.

To see the wholly specious nature of the argument here it is worthwhile following Friedman in his development of this line of thinking in relation to the Fair Employment Practices Commission (FEPC) introduced by President Roosevelt in 1941 to prevent discrimination in government industries. His argument is that this sort of interference, once it had a broader application than just public works, 'clearly involves interference with the freedom of individuals to enter into voluntary contracts with one another' (111). His claim is that this legislation confuses two types of harm, the physical force or coercion he calls 'positive harm', and the inability 'to find mutually acceptable contracts' (112), or the refusal to buy something because of my 'preference for blues singers over opera singers', for example, which he calls 'negative harm'. 'Positive harm' is something a government committed to freedom should prevent, while the negative harm caused by peoples' preferences, even prejudices, is not something a government should concern itself with. His example runs as follows:

> consider a situation in which there are grocery stores serving a neighborhood inhabited by people who have a strong aversion to being waited on by Negro clerks. Suppose one of the grocery stores has a vacancy for a clerk and the first applicant qualified in other respects happens to be a Negro. Let us suppose that as a result of the law the store is required to hire him. The effect of this action will be to reduce the business done by this store and to impose losses on the owner. If the preference of the community is strong enough, it may even cause the store to close. When the owner of the store hires white clerks in preference to Negroes in the absence of the law, he may not be expressing any preference or prejudice or taste of his own. He may simply be transmitting the tastes of the community. He is, as it were, producing the

services for the consumers that the consumers are willing to pay for. Nonetheless, he is harmed, and indeed may be the only one harmed appreciably, by a law which prohibits him from engaging in this activity, that is, prohibits him from pandering to the tastes of the community for having a white rather than a Negro clerk. (111–2)

Returning to the difference in preference for blues over opera, he argues that while a community's taste for music might 'harm' the opera singer, 'this kind of harm does not involve any involuntary exchange or an imposition of costs or granting of benefits to third parties' and as such there is 'no case whatsoever for using government to avoid this negative kind of harm' (113). What is extraordinary in these few pages is Friedman's equation of racism with musical preference. It is just tough for the opera singer that the community, or market, prefers blues, just as it is tough for the black person that the market prefers white people. By extension we are expected to believe that while the preference for music doesn't involve involuntary exchange or an imposition of costs the same can be said for the racist refusal to employ someone. But can the refusal to employ someone due to the colour of their skin really not be seen as the imposition of costs when this person may not be able to secure earnings? And how can it be said that this involves no involuntary exchange when the victim of racism is forced to secure work beneath their qualifications and experience because it is the only one open to a black person. Here again we can see the incredibly impoverished sense of freedom that free marketeers work with. This is because an environment of discrimination doesn't impact in any way upon a person's *formal* freedom.

This effectively means that the 'positive harm' inflicted on the shopkeeper's takings trumps the 'negative harm' inflicted on the black man because the communal victimisation he experiences is not coercion, but simply the inability to secure a mutually beneficial contract, which, according the free marketeers, he could theoretically secure elsewhere (which brings to mind the infamous 'On yer bike' response attributed to Norman Tebbit, Margaret Thatcher's Employment Secretary, to arguments that race riots in Handsworth and Brixton in 1981 were fuelled by lack of employment amongst Britain's black youth). Or, put another way, the loss of the shopkeeper's potential earnings as a result of government intervention is of greater importance than the loss of the black person's potential earnings due to intervention by private and free individuals acting in concert to impose their racist beliefs. This raises a number of questions, not least: Is coercion only coercion when it is supported by law or is mandatory? And is intervention in private affairs only called intervention when it is enacted by the state? If so, why? As was shown in the last chapter, because positive economics has no understanding of psychology or sociology in any meaningful sense these questions of non-governmental coercion or intervention not only don't arise, but can't arise. They are unintelligible within this closed system of thought.

As long as there is no law stipulating a black person cannot own property or cannot be employed, it is perfectly acceptable according to this argument for a person to be discriminated against if that is what the market wants. It is perfectly acceptable if the unacknowledged social and political bias that is built into any and every existing market works against a black person by not permitting them to earn or own to their full potential, as long as there isn't a law that purposefully engineers such inequality. The argument assumes that there will always be some kind of a job somewhere in a free market, and the fact that someone might have to settle for a more menial, or less well paid, let alone less secure, or less healthy one, is only what the impersonal market wants; and a market remains impersonal even if it puts up signs saying 'No Niggers'.

Friedman's wonderfully liberal response to racism, then, is not government protection for the victims, but a free market of ideas modelled on the free market for goods and services. What needs to be done is convince people, he argues, that racism is wrong, and for this we need free, unlicenced, unregulated airwaves. Of course, Friedman's free market in ideas remains haunted by the communism that permeates all his work. The free market in ideas again assumes as real a non-existent, utopic space for the fully equal exchange of beliefs and theories, a space where every participant has formal, and therefore equal access to the means of mental production, as they have formal, and therefore equal access to the means of material production in the bucolic Nirvana he calls the '*free private enterprise exchange economy*'. If this basic communist ideal of perfect parity amongst individuals who all have a formal share in the means of production and circulation of ideas, goods and services is not assumed, then this argument makes no sense because once more it purposefully leaves out any sense of social bias. The conclusion is that the dominant ideas are those the market deems good, but this is amoral pragmatism turned relativism. There is absolutely nothing in this advocacy of a purely economic defence against discrimination that would in any way protect minorities against wholesale persecution. The only thing that would need to remain in place to satisfy Friedman is the formal defence of the free use and disposal of private property. For those that end up without any, if it hasn't happened by state decree, then it's just tough luck.

The argument assumes that a free market in private property and private employment will always counter discrimination, but this is because Friedman has little conception, or interest, in how a free market can still produce collectivist behaviour that is extremely damaging to minority interests and could indeed produce an authoritarian regime equivalent to anything built by a collectivist state. In this system there is little sense for the cultivation and active production of social bias. There is little understanding, as we saw in the previous chapter, of how a particular worldview or ideology might be actively managed in the interests of those who most directly benefit from the system. Because proponents of free market economics prefer to abstract themselves from the social complexities that underpin human behaviour, or rather their theories of market dynamics demands this abstraction, it is perfectly plausible to assume that the market can be this panacea. Despite his use of historical examples as evidence in support of his argument Friedman in effect brackets out history. He deploys the odd historical example as 'evidence' for his argument, but history, understood as the sedimentation of beliefs, practices and social relations, has been effectively removed from his communist idyll. The formal equality of positive economics that can only exist in some unrealisable future papers over the substantial inequalities of history that persist in the present. There is a symbolic violence here that has a certain kinship with other revolutionary movements that base themselves in communist ideals: the institution of the Party or the Market represents the overcoming of inequalities (history), meaning that any remaining grievance is either illusionary – even delusionary – or reactionary, counter-revolutionary, and therefore criminal. In refusing to accept the persistence of very real inequalities and the legitimacy of grievances arising from them, Friedman situates a violence at the heart of his utopia that permits a great deal of harm in the name of freedom. Despite Friedman's writings existing very much on the periphery of current economic thinking they remain central for free market ideologues, and represent very real dangers in idiotism's drive towards the privatisation of life.

Only when we understand that a free market is never in fact free, but is always already historically skewed in favour of those with the most economic power (capital) can we countenance the idea that a government might be required to intervene in order to protect the equality constitutionally mandated, but not necessarily economically, socially or politically instituted. The US government is charged with fulfilling the promise that the US constitution is based on. This is not a purely formal freedom or formal equality where it matters little if people are substantially constrained and unequal. The fact that Friedman argues against positive harm means that even for him the government cannot solely operate at the level of the formal and abstract, but must pay attention to what is actually happening to people in their lives. All that Friedman does is simply draw an arbitrary line in the sand to argue that the state should only intervene to ensure the physical security of private property. All other kinds of intervention, including protection against the discrimination that disables people from securing property in the first place verges on totalitarianism. In the end the only moral obligation the shopkeeper has is to give the customers what they want, and the only moral obligation the state should observe is facilitating the shopkeeper's freedom, in this instance, to pander to prejudice. If the free market in private property has no other moral criterion than giving the customer what they want in the pursuit of maximum economic productivity – for this is all the rhetoric of formal freedom and equality means – then there is absolutely no reason why idiotism as a form of politics, or Friedman's particular version of depoliticisation could not result in the sort of dispossession and persecution that free-marketeers ordinarily associate with the most doctrinaire forms of collectivism. Simply because Friedman wishes away bias by positing the free market as a heavenly space of rational purity does not mean that bias no longer exists. His work is thus in keeping with the philosophical and religious cults that have sought to do away with the messiness, ambiguity, and partiality of physical existence in favour of a disembodied and disembedded notion of reason. Only by abstracting pluralism from its socio-historical conditions can Friedman make an argument for pluralism untainted by bias. It is odd, then, that so many advocates of the free market dogma call themselves realists when reality is so carefully excised from the model.

MANAGERIALISM

A contemporary of Friedman was Elmer E. Schattschneider who once famously wrote that 'the flaw in the pluralist heaven is that the heavenly chorus sings with a strong upper-class accent' (1960:35). To understand the significance of this phrase today, and the relevance of class for analysing the organisational bias of idiotism, class analysis needs to be re-thought in relation to idiotism as a global(ising) condition. This potentially means two countervailing things. First it is important to think of class formations beyond the borders of particular nations, that is, to think about idiotism being driven by a TCC. Entirely counter to the idealism of the free marketeers, an analysis of the TCC shows how the extension of the economic realm in the form of deregulation, privatisation and financialisation absolutely requires social and political intervention in the form of direct action on the part of politicians, civil servants and managers, amongst others, who, in addition to capitalists provide the necessary conditions for the free flow of global capital. Secondly, with this global management of a system demanding the participation of a number of differing social actors from a range of institutions and social sectors, thereby possibly making the category of social or economic class too fuzzy to be useful, it is also necessary to ask whether or not, with the rise of managerialism, a form of social organisation has emerged that has superseded both socialism and capitalism, and that we might therefore have to abandon a class analysis altogether.

Such a position is set out in Willard F. Enteman's *Managerialism: The Emergence of a New Ideology*. In this book Enteman contends that managerialism has not only taken over from capitalism and socialism, but has actually replaced democracy as well. It is therefore quite a radical theory of depoliticisation. He can offer this argument primarily because of the way he respectively defines these three modes of social organisation in terms of atomism, organicism, and process. While the first two are perhaps obvious – capitalism is atomistic because it assumes the individual consumer as its basic unit, while socialism is organic for its commitment to a totality that supposedly transcends individuals – democracy is defined in terms of process because Entemann views it primarily as a means 'for resolving disputes and conflicts' (1993:39) that emerge among citizens. While there are problems with these definitions, not least because the market can be seen to be a process for resolving disputes (see Friedman above), they do permit Entemann to differentiate managerialism from them. He writes: 'The managerialist society is not one which responds to the needs, desires, and wishes of a majority of its citizens. In the managerialist society, influence is exercised through organizations. The society responds to whatever the managements of various organizations can gain in their transactions with each other' (154). Managerialism, for Entemann, is thus the sublation of atomism, organicism and process. It incorporates individuals but only as they are represented by managerial units; such units can be organic wholes with which members might strongly identify, but they never come to be, nor claim to be a social totality; and the system operates through the interaction and decision-making of the *managers* of these social units (not the units themselves). For Entemann, this means that society 'is nothing more than the summation of the decisions and transactions which have been made by the managements of the organizations' (159). It is 'a lethal challenge to democracy' (159), he argues, not only because it is not individuals making decisions, but also because without management you cannot participate in transactions. This is then compounded by Entemann's contention that the management of each unit primarily seeks to secure the best deal for itself in the first instance and only secondly for its members. Managerialism thus becomes a self-reproducing system in which management is always at an advantage.

While Entemann's book is very good in many ways, not least because it is one of the few that tries to get to the radical nature of what has been happening over the last 30 years, there are a number of problems with it. He argues that managerialism is a name for 'deep social change, not a name for attitudinal shifts' (156), and in this I would have to agree. The shift to a global free market and the forms of micro- and macro-governance that have emerged with it are not superficial phenomena. And while the production and reproduction of managerialism clearly demands an engagement with the systems theory of Niklas Luhmann and Immanuel Wallerstein, my own treatment of which will need to be reserved for further work, the problem with Entemann's approach lies predominantly in his definition of the systems that managerialism has supposedly supplanted. That managerialism has superseded socialism, is to some degree plausible, given the sorry state that socialism finds itself in, but that does not mean that socialism is irrelevant, in fact quite the contrary is the case. Socialism only appears irrelevant because the complexity of socialist systems is constantly denigrated or ignored in favour of the usual caricature of socialism as totalitarianism. In this way Entemann sticks with the definition most readily deployed by capitalists: socialism equates to the transcendence and negation of the individual and the particular on the journey to some higher Good (which always turns out, of course, to be Evil). With regard to democracy there can be little doubt that this has also been superseded as is demonstrated by the power of the new aristocracy or financial oligarchy, but again Entemann works with very established conceptions of a supposedly liberal *demos* that, while dominant in political science, cannot be said to exhaust the term. But the biggest problem lies with his definition of capitalism as atomistic. Such a definition permits him to argue that social organisation via individuals has now been replaced by social organisation via managerial units, but in doing this he uses a conception of social organisation (atomism) that he argues is no longer valid. In other words, to say that we have moved beyond capitalism he uses a definition of it that is completely inadequate to understand how it works. Capitalism has never and will never run as an aggregation of individual choices. This is, rather, its central fantasy. Capitalism, and what I am calling idiotism, posits the individual and personal consumer choice as the founding unit of social organisation, but all the while it operates through units of social influence or, in the language of chapter 1, the referential totalities of specific worlds. As was discussed in the previous chapter, there is absolutely no such thing as a purely individual choice, or a purely innate desire, and even the most radical projections of future goals emerge out of a world that frames those decisions. Despite capitalism's claims to the privileging of individuality it is not immune to facticity and the social influence of ideology or what Heidegger called 'das Man' – the largely anonymous tastes and preferences of wider groupings. Capitalism, nevertheless, consistently disavows the fact that it is a complex, but very large ideological system aiming at the collective (re)production of desire as much as the production of goods.

What managerialism offers us, then, especially as it is set out by Entemann is a way of describing not the surpassing of capitalism, but the very mechanism by which the contemporary form of capitalism (idiotism) both extends itself beyond the economic realm and broadens its social reach. 'Social choice', he writes, 'arises out of group managerial transactions. Effectively there is no direct linkage between social choice and individual preferences. At the same time, there is no identifiable overarching social personality' (Entemann 1993:191). Managerialism as both a descriptive and explanatory model is attractive, therefore, not only because it displaces the central myth of idiotism regarding the primacy of individual preference, replacing it with the reality of managerial transactions, but because in this it offers a means for thinking how idiotism, as a fundamentally economic dogma, might be able to extend itself across every aspect of social life. With regard to the latter, though, it is necessary to challenge Entemann's claim that there is no overarching personality that might be said to guide or shape the transactions amongst units, thereby bringing it in line with the argument that the system that managerialism manages is one driven by the interests of the TCC. To be sure, there is no God, monarch, or dictator, no *person* that determines our choices, nor is there an essential human nature that drives social choice in a specific direction, but there is no need to establish some kind of sovereign personality to be able to argue that choice is motivated by forces beyond the specific dynamics that determine relations between social units. In the opening chapter it has already been shown how the impersonality of 'das Man' becomes the measure of the everyday activities – choices and decisions – that absorb us. The meaningfulness of our world is not a subject, but it still directs our every move. So to be able to use Entemann's insights to account for the rise and spread of idiotism it is necessary to explain how transactions are shaped not just by the specific concerns and interests at play in the interactions between particular units, but how transactions become entrained towards the advancement of a very specific social organisation known as the free market: as Schattschneider also reminded us, there is no such thing as neutral organisation because '*organization is the mobilization of bias*' (1960:71). The only question that remains is how to explain the organisational bias with regard to idiotism.

Entemann's critique of atomism coupled with his rejection of any overarching social determinant permits him to rather absurdly declare that 'capitalist assumptions [...] are irrelevant to the advanced industrialized societies of the late twentieth century' (1993:155). In speaking of the irrelevance of capitalism he is not only assuming capitalism to be atomistic, but is also accepting another nonsensical premise from positive economics that the economy is deterministic, or that the capitalist system is determined by purely economic, rather than social or psychological factors. Because Entemann perceives a capacity for 'effective discretion' (169) in the current system, and positive economics to some degree excludes discretion, he claims further grounds for the supersession of capitalism on this point. But with capitalism gone he has very little means left to account for how power operates around this capacity for discretion, or decision-making, and thereby to explain its bias. Accounts of capitalism need not assume some overarching personality for capitalism's continuation. In his excellent study of global capital William I. Robinson argues for what he calls a 'recursive effect' that benefits a particular dominant class, but that 'the structures of the global economy come about as the unplanned outcome of strategic decisions taken by thousands of firms [...], but these structures then present themselves to capitalist and other social agents as a reality conducive to further actions toward trans-nationalization' (2004:69). There is no 'personality' commanding or directing the system, but there is a strategy, or an interlacing of strategies, that produces a centripetal force in terms of capitalist accumulation and a definite direction for future strategy.

Returning to Entemann, he does list features that might make one particular managerial unit stronger or weaker, and includes factors such as 'membership size' and 'organic behaviour', but surely the key factor is what he calls 'discretionary wealth' (1993:161), or the amount of resources (capital) that each unit has at its disposal. The shift from a commercial to an industrial and then a financial capitalism is the perfect example of the direction given by discretionary wealth. Unfortunately, Entemann does not develop this point. This is a shame because wealth is not just one factor amongst others. It is *the* factor determining in a very large part the efficacy of the other factors Entemann includes such as 'public rhetoric', defined as public relations, or image and information management. To paraphrase Marx and Engels in *The German Ideology*, those who have control over material production also have control over mental, or what is sometimes now called immaterial production, and when material production becomes increasingly a matter of immaterial production – as images, messages, information, and data – the link between wealth, public rhetoric and social efficacy becomes even more pronounced. Thus the idea that discretionary wealth is just one factor amongst others is incorrect and seems to be downplayed in order to permit him to prematurely pronounce the surpassing of capitalism.

Running counter to Entemann is Richard Sennett's argument in *The Culture of the New Capitalism* that managers have in fact been disabused. Here he is arguing against the kinds of managerialism associated with top-down, iron cage, as he calls them, bureaucracies. Linking this to changes in capitalism, and in particular changes to the relationship between capitalism and the state, Sennett speaks of the emergence of a 'lateral power' (2006:39) made up of industrialists and increasingly investors. With regard to the explicit control of old-style bureaucratic managers, Sennett writes: 'Investors became active judges [and] the leveraged buyout meant that investors could make or break corporations while its management stood helplessly by' (39). This kind of activity, which has become increasingly prevalent with the financialisation of the economy, indicates that the power of capitalists and of capital is undiminished, but idiotism *is wholly dependent* on the rise of managers to depoliticise interactions by subsuming each unit within the logic of the market. This subsumption is highly differentiated dependent upon the traditional relationship each unit has to the workings of capital, but managerialism facilitates this alignment due to the influence of discretionary wealth on managerial transactions. Entemann's insights are, therefore, very important but would be much more useful if instead of claiming capitalism to be over – based on a spurious definition of how capitalism works that only the most blinkered economists would now recognise – he argued that managerialism represents the logical culmination of an economic system that requires all kinds of social actors to be fully dominant. In other words, the strategies and decisions that have created the latest phase of capitalism are not only made by corporate boards, but by countless management teams that respond to the new 'reality'.

There is a strong sense in Entemann that managerialism is not committed to any specific form of social organisation. Instead, managerialism is cybernetic, a system of self-reproducing units that do what is necessary to prosper by bargaining, negotiating, accommodating, challenging, and all without being determined by some pre-given, external agenda. However, each one of these units exists within an environment in which discretionary wealth, or capital, remains a strongly determining factor in the relative strength or weakness of units. This has clearly been the case with unions, for example, whose management has had to take up much greater proximity to the managers of capital in order to ensure their survival. Over the course of the last century, unions and labour organisations have made enormous gains for working men and women in terms of pay and conditions, health and safety, maternity and paternity rights, and pensions, but these are also features that have stabilised capital (at least in ideological, if not strictly economic terms) in its shift from the extraction of absolute surplus value (slavery), to relative surplus value (wage labour and welfarism). Union managers need to attend to members' needs in order to maintain strength in numbers, but they must also pay heed to the requirements of capital to avoid being legislated out of existence. A more cynical approach and one that I do not espouse would be Tiqqun's argument that 'the workers' movement has always been the vehicle for Capital-Utopia' (2011:32). The fact that the system is managerialist and not atomistic despite the ideological desire to posit the individual as the founding unit does not mean it is not capitalism. Where welfarism carried a trace of socialist thinking within it, managerialism is the victory of capitalism without contamination. Managerialism is the means by which capital maximises the influence of discretionary wealth throughout the entire social field, turning conflict into arbitration, dissensus into negotiation, and heterogeneity into dialogue; all of which are examples of depoliticisation as any radical ideological difference is gradually excised from managerial transactions. But capitalism is so riven with contradictions related to wage-labour, growth, sustainability, and human dignity, to name only a few that it requires a concerted effort across all elements of social life to retain its prominence. As was shown in the previous chapter it is not sustained as the result of naked and rational economic laws, but by (potentially irrational) confidence and (regularly irrational) desire. It is a belief system maintained through the observation of doctrinal rules and the propagation of the faith in every institution, whether public or private. Managerialism, then, is nothing but the maintenance and transmission of the capitalist liturgy to all parts of society. It is not a new ideology, as Entemann claims, but the fine tuning of a hegemonic process that has emerged over many decades.

The success of capitalism, supported by the power of discretionary wealth, has been its ability to infiltrate all areas of life, something that various commentators have referred to as biopolitics. What we need to take from Entemann, therefore, is an analysis of capitalism in which we no longer think of power being exercised solely by capitalists, as either industrialists or investors, but by a range of social actors and institutions that broadens the scope of the strategic elements necessary for its continuation and expansion, and as capitalism globalises it is increasingly necessary to see managerialism operating in a transnational context. The problem, of course, is that the new form of managerialism that has replaced the old style, top-down bureaucracies, and the globalisation that has replaced the nation-state, imperial phase of capitalism are both understood to be decentralising phenomena, and it is difficult to maintain both a notion of decentralisation *and* a concept of the hierarchical power essential for class analysis. That we can have a concept of radical decentralisation and still conceive of power has been shown by Michael Hardt and Antonio Negri (2000), but the persistence of discretionary wealth and its tendency to reside in specific national or regional spaces, despite arguments pertaining to the fluidity of capital, disproves Hardt and Negri's argument in favour of a smooth, centreless, networked power. Capitalism is certainly networked, and managerialism offers another version of this networked power, but it remains hierarchical and has a centring effect, so to speak. While partly supporting Hardt and Negri's analysis of empire, Robinson is much closer to my own position of 'transnational realism' (Curtis 2006:174) regarding the financial and military dominance of the United States, arguing that: *'The empire of capital is headquartered in Washington'*.

THE TRANSNATIONAL CAPITALIST CLASS

There is a tendency to think that hierarchy, authority, and hence power, demand centralisation, but we only have to look at the modern military (and the US military, in particular) to realise this is not the case. Decentralisation in the military is taking two forms. The first is the privatisation of 'security'. Here the government's monopoly on violence is outsourced to private corporations who provide mercenaries to supplement the regular army. But supplement is not quite the right term given that private mercenaries in their varying 'security' details often outnumber the regular troops, forming something akin to a capitalist Praetorian Guard (Hirst 2001:98). What is more, the decentralisation that comes with the privatisation of war is increased when the number of companies involved is taken into account. According to Jeremy Scahill (2007), while Blackwater are the biggest name in privatised security, the Iraq war also saw other firms such as Control Risk Group, DynCorp, Erinys, Aegis, ArmourGroup, Hart, Kroll and Steele Foundation (76) deploy mercenaries to the area. This is compounded, or we have an additional element of decentralisation when such firms are 'granted sweeping immunity for its operations' (Scahill 2007:150), as happened with Blackwater under Paul Bremer's Coalition Provisional Authority Order Number 17 on 27 June 2004. This is logistical, executive and judicial decentralisation in relation to war fighting, but there can be no doubt that this all functions within a very clear hierarchy, or chain of command. It may not be the rigid Taylorist pyramid of traditional management; it is far too lateral in its organisation and may have a number of peaks, but it is very far from flat or smooth. This is also the case with the second form of military decentralisation. Since the development of cybernetics, and much to Norbert Wiener's distaste, it has been central to what has been called the Revolution in Military Affairs (RMA) to develop the capacity for war-fighters to swarm, that is, respond with ever greater rapidity and precision to changes in the battle space – something that is also allied to Network-Centric Warfare, or Full Spectrum Dominance. It is also the capacity to produce 'spontaneous cooperation' (DeLanda 1991:59) and the elimination of the 'friction' 'responsible for delays, bottlenecks and machine breakdowns' (60). Here what is important is that each node in the system, each war-fighter, has the capability to feed information into the system that might enable effective and decisive moves in response to an enemy. In this scenario the old assumptions about command and control go out of the window, but this does not mean that authority, or unity of purpose goes with it. Non-linearity is not anarchy, but a more complex form of order.

Returning to the issue of management it is Sennett that provides the best analogy for the kinds of decentralised, flexible organisation that is both in keeping with a class analysis of late, or post-Fordist capitalism, and Entemann's conception of managerialist decision-making understood as the interaction of numerous relatively autonomous units. In talking about the 'new institutional architecture' Sennett brings to mind the 'uniquely modern machine' known generically as the MP3 player (2006:47). This machine can modify sequence, programme, function, and content, depending on the mood, activity, and location of its user, and as such is the perfect model of flexible organisation, and yet in an MP3 player, 'the laser in the central processing unit is boss. While there is random access to material, flexible performance is possible only because the central processing unit is in control of the whole' (51). For Sennett this means that in the world of work, groups are given autonomy to deliver quick, flexible results, but the terms of internal competition are all centrally set (52). Here what passes as decentralisation, or has a number of characteristics that can be read as being decentralised, also contains elements that remain understandable within traditional Taylorist and Fordist conceptions of authority, power and control. Managerialism, then, is certainly on the rise, and colours all aspects of life under late capitalism, but this is precisely the point, it remains capitalist. It may be decentralised and without an overarching personality directing it, but it does have a centripetal effect as the relatively autonomous units necessarily align themselves with discretionary wealth.

What Entemann allows us to see, then, is the social constructed as the interaction of differing managerial units. Wealth is maintained and reproduced according to the neoliberal logic of markets, privatisation, commodities, competition, financialisation, and customer service, and for each managerial unit to survive it must play according to the rules that gives it its particular form of legitimacy, but also by the rules that determine its strength or weakness in relation to the accumulation of discretionary wealth. There may indeed be greater autonomy, but autonomy is secured only if it results in greater systemic efficiencies, and by this is meant the reduction of friction in the flow of capital. All areas must comply in this new independence. This means that one fortunate by-product of managerialism in relation to the particular form of accumulation of discretionary wealth that currently holds sway is that through its centripetal function, in which it increasingly aligns an array of social units with the dogma of privatised solutions, it also has a centrifugal effect on resistance by breaking up or dissolving other factors that might influence transactions between units. Managerialism is in effect a form of niche-disciplining in the realm of production analogous to the niche-marketing in the realm of consumption, and as such it is a key feature of political idiotism.

This means that decentralisation in itself does not counter power, nor does it necessarily diminish authority. Indeed, given that the military is a perfect example of decentralisation being used in pursuit of a unitary goal, it cannot be said that decentralisation automatically undermines the potential for authoritarianism either. In the same way that depoliticisation remains a deeply *political* phenomenon, decentralisation is profoundly *centralizing*: it is the most efficient means for furthering the dogmatic social goals of idiotism, namely the extension of the free market, the mediation of the commodity, and the privatisation of anything held in common. Thus, decentralisation as it pertains to idiotism is anything but democratic, despite regularly dressing itself up in democratic garb. When an establishment figure such as Simon Johnson (2010), a former chief economist of the IMF, writes a book setting out in detail how we can legitimately speak of a financial oligarchy – primarily an oligarchy of bankers – holding complete sway over Washington, and therefore the political process of the most powerful nation in the world, it is difficult not to agree with Entemann that democracy has passed away, but the same cannot be said for capitalism.

As much as it is essential to think of depoliticisation as a political process, it is necessary to also find a way of conceptualising the seeming contradiction of an oligarchy functioning through a process of decentralisation. The presence of a financial oligarchy at the top of the political tree suggests that we have indeed moved away from democracy, but not that we have entered the neutral territory that Entemann calls managerialism. Managerialism is the method through which idiotism extends itself socially and culturally, but it is not neutral. In a plutocracy, discretionary wealth becomes the invisible hand (sometimes the invisible fist) that entrains the decentralised decisions emerging out of the transactions between the management of different social units. The state of the university as an institution is very revealing in this regard. Managers of humanities departments find their jobs easier, i.e. defending the work of their staff, if that work can be shown to fit with the increasingly corporate model that is being adopted across the UK's higher education system. Here, for example, work in cultural studies transforms into work in the creative industries. This is because the managers of the university can get more out of their transactions with other relevant managerial units such as the research councils and the Department for Education, if they can be shown to be directly contributing to the economy in a manner in keeping with the drift towards the free market. And this is because the managerial team known as the Cabinet can get more from its negotiations with the managers of capital if they can make the country more amenable to its free flow. The managers of capital cannot extend the free market and the requisite thinking that will allow the free market to flourish by imposing its will, or rather it can do this only in countries where the population are already so politically and socially disenfranchised that resistance is difficult. In advanced capitalist countries the increasingly authoritarian dogma of a free market and privatised solutions is advanced by the power of discretionary wealth trickling through the niche-disciplining of a managerial system that while decentralised and comprised of differentiated social units nevertheless gravitates towards a unitary social goal.

This highlighting of the connection between the social, political and economic, as well as the local, national and transnational in the complex process of managerial decision-making necessitates some closing remarks on the TCC. While Entemann's analysis of managerialism is essential if we are to understand that decision-making does not emerge from a purely capitalist or economic class, that is, decision-making needs to be understood as a diverse social process, the fact that we live in a plutocracy in which discretionary wealth has a gravitational pull on that process permits us to think of decentralised decision-making that culminates in the dominance of a single worldview. As I have already noted, Sklair's analysis of the TCC is compatible with Entemann's theory of managerialism, if we accept that the emergence of managerialism does not necessarily mean the end of capitalism. For Sklair the TCC is made up of diverse economic, political and social actors, all of whom 'partake differentially in recognizable global patterns of capital accumulation, consuming, and thinking' (2000:12), and here globalisation is understood both as the physical extension of conditions best suited to the advancement of the TCC as well as a form of governance or management through which those conditions are first established and then maintained. Globalisation, writes Sklair, 'means transnational practices in which transnational corporations […] strive to maximize private profits globally […] without special reference to the interests (real or imagined) of their countries of citizenship', and this is in keeping with Entemann's analysis of managerialism because: 'The [TCC] mobilizes the resources necessary to accomplish this objective [by] working through a variety of social institutions [units], including state and quasi-state agencies, the professions, and the mass media' (82).

Here, it is what Sklair calls the 'technopols' that are essential to the management of the system. Technopols are those managers of social units that understand their interests are best served by aligning themselves with the influence of discretionary wealth, whether that be the government minister who introduces laws to deregulate publicly owned assets; the doctor who supports moves towards private financing; or the head of a humanities department who has come to accept the 'reality' that all research needs to be monetised. In the specifically political realm this means 'technopols need to develop a political agenda to establish a cosmopolitan vision that locks in their countries to free markets, international trade agreements, and globalisation, and to create political openings to bring all important social groups on side for 'national' development' (Sklair 2000:138). The current assault on higher education in the UK, and the humanities in particular, is a perfect example of this kind of national development. At present, the university is one of the rare institutions that isn't completely in lock-step with the new common sense. A central feature of idiotism, then, is the effort being made by technopols and managers to stifle dissent and dislodge any friction that undermines the capacity to align units with discretionary wealth.

What is interesting about Sklair's analysis of the TCC is that it is a social, rather than a purely political or economic grouping, but to think of it in relation to the diverse units of Entemann's managerialism we also need to think of the TCC in terms of the 'fractionation' discussed by Robinson (2004). For Robinson, because capitalism is a fundamentally competitive system this makes 'any real unity in the global ruling class impossible' (46). Again, this means there is no overarching personality directing things because the TCC actually comprises fractions that sometimes work with each other, sometimes against each other, but the overall effect is the continuation – sometimes the transmutation – of a system that always benefits what he calls a 'hegemonic fraction'. In his analysis the TCC has a number of fractions each of which at different historical conjunctures in the development of capitalism have been hegemonic. Thus we have seen the fraction of industrial capital take over from the earlier more dominant fraction of commercial or mercantile capital, which has in turn been superseded by the fraction of financial capital. Robinson also notes the suggestion in some quarters that we can determine a fraction of information capital relating to the emergence of the new dotcom companies (37). His main point here, however, is to argue that globalisation also entails competition between national, regional and transnational fractions whose interests lie in specific forms of territorialisation and deter-ritorialisation, but it is also essential to see Entemann's managerial units as fractions of the TCC, especially when the management of these units is coupled to the movement of discretionary wealth: there is the fraction that ensures the requisite national laws are in place to maximise the free flow of transnational capital; there is the fraction that manages labour relations so as to minimise disruption; there is the fraction that legitimises certain forms of knowledge over others; there is the fraction that circulates the discourses and images that reproduce the new common sense; there is the fraction that pathologises the non-passive and prescribes a pharmaceutical rather than a social cure; there is the fraction that polices non-compliant, or rogue states, and in the process generates huge investment opportunities. These are only a few of the social units that can also be seen as fractions of the TCC. Of course, the educational fraction can never become hegemonic because it will never have sufficient discretionary wealth at its disposal, but it is absolutely essential that these units and their managers accept the ruling dogma and open themselves to the workings of free market capital if they are to retain relative strength with regard to discretionary wealth. A managerialist view of the TCC also permits us to see fractions that are both national and transnational at the same time, such as the globalising technopols of national governments who must 'look after' their own populations, whilst also securing the conditions that most benefit global capital and the free market. The TCC is, therefore, not a class in the old sense of a social rank. It is not unitary, as was noted above. The TCC necessarily comprises units from all social levels. This is the only way that idiotism can take hold of the entire social field, but having said that, it remains hierarchical and can be said to contain fractional elites, groupings that Alain Joxe has called a new aristocracy (2002), or those with greatest proximity to the centres of discretionary wealth.

Thus, idiotism as it pertains to politics is this dual track of depoliticisation. In the first instance it is the reduction of the concerns of traditional politics to market relations. Secondly, it is the management of society in accordance with the interests of the hegemonic capitalist fraction, and it does not need the direction of an overarching personality for it to be authoritarian. The in-built bias towards discretionary wealth, and the managerialist organisation of the social according to the rules that best suit that wealth, are sufficient conditions to produce a dogma that has the same unity of purpose supposed to be only achievable under collectivist conditions. But because this dogma requires the alignment of a vast array of social units for its success the process of depoliticisa- tion can never be complete. I return to this in the final chapter, but here it is important to stress that each unit is a node in a network, but these are not nodes akin to individual computers in relation to the internet where loss of one computer does not prevent the circulation of information. This is a metaphor that has gained a certain currency, but managerialism tells us something different. It tells us that each node or unit is absolutely essential to the running of the system and the flooding of the social field. This means that each unit comprises a site for repoliticisation and that political activity still has targets. Power is decentred, but it is not entirely without location. Furthermore, because managers have to pay some attention to those they manage, and not just ensure they have been sufficiently disciplined to autonomously pursue market solutions, political activity can still be effective around these locations. Also, in Entemann's analysis of the relative strength and weakness of social units, the only factor that could at all challenge discretionary wealth is membership numbers. Given that it is safe to say that the poor greatly outnumber the rich, turning towards the poor is one way in which the influence of discretionary wealth might be challenged. This is not to say with Hardt and Negri that '*The poor itself is power*' (2000:157), but that the turn towards the poor, by those who feel ideologically impoverished when faced with the doctrine that only the marketable has value, is one way in which Jodi Dean's call for an alternative solidarity can yet be built.

5
Idiotism and Culture

If managerialism is the technique that enables idiotism to flood the social field, this must also require the entrainment of culture in line with the ideology of privatisation. If society is taken to be the organisation of the institutions and units of which it is comprised, culture must be understood as the meaningful practices that animate this structure. The alignment of culture with the organisation of society is therefore necessary if the worldview such organisation promotes is to appear to be a democratically evolved, 'organic' common sense rather than an ideology imposed by an oligarchy influenced by discretionary wealth. That this is perfectly understood by idiotism's chief ideologues is evident from a comment Margaret Thatcher made in an interview published in the *Sunday Times* on 1 May 1981 where her Randian influence was already clear to see. In it she complains:

> What's irritated me about the whole direction of politics in the last 30 years is that it's always been towards the collectivist society. People have forgotten about the personal society. And they say: do I count, do I matter? To which the short answer is, yes. And therefore, it isn't that I set out on economic policies; it's that I set out really to change the approach, and changing the economics is the means of changing that approach. If you change the approach you really are after the heart and soul of the nation. Economics are the method; the object is to change the heart and soul.

What Thatcher here refers to as the heart and soul of the nation is the culture that was still 'tainted' with postwar collectivism, as Hayek suggested it would be. The soul thus represents those elements of culture not yet aligned to the ideology of idiotism. Before talking specifically about the 'personal society' that Thatcher sought to cultivate it is important to say a little more about how the soul can be thought in relation to culture as well as how the soul can be both affected and effective, that is, how it might be changed and in turn bring about a change in people's beliefs and practices.

THE SOUL

In his book *The Soul at Work* Franco Berardi describes the soul as 'the vital breath that converts biological matter into an animated body' (2009:21). In a similar vein I would like to describe culture as that animating element that converts institutions into the living social body we call a world. While social institutions give culture a certain objectivity or shape, culture is not reducible to these institutional functions. Without this other element the world becomes inanimate. However, given that culture understood as a way of life must be seen as the creation and circulation of meaning, or the distribution of sense-making practices, *and* that the production of sense is an interminable and infinitely creative process, culture must also be seen as the site of perpetual conflict and disagreement regarding the nature of the world we live in. The problem, however, is the polyglottal culture that liberal institutions were supposed to protect has given way to the 'panlogism' of neo-liberalism where cultural heterogeneity has been repackaged as market differentiation. In effect idiotism prefers an efficient swarm of digitised consumers to the curious, many-headed chimera of the cultural multitude.

For Berardi, then, the capture of the soul by the post-Fordist, neo-liberal regime is an essential step in the consolidation of the capitalist system. A key feature here is the development of 'cognitive labour', or 'immaterial labour'. With advanced economies increasingly turning to services, knowledge and information, capitalism morphs into what Berardi calls 'Semiocapitalism', a regime that 'takes the mind, language and creativity as its primary tools for the production of value' (2009:21). This is how the soul and culture are now set to work; our imagination, aesthetic sensibility, and the sociality that is the site of ingenuity and inventiveness are all folded into the production of economic value. But this is important for another reason. The soul has not only become a new source of productive value, its capture has also meant the incorporation of that which had previously been allowed to remain external to the regime of accumulation. As Berardi notes: 'In the history of capitalism the body was disciplined and put to work while the soul was left on hold, unoccupied, neglected' (115). The soul could be left to itself so long as the body turned up each day for work, but in this indifference to the soul capitalism exposed itself to a source of resistance because the 'overturning of the body's submission to domination became possible precisely because the soul remained separate from it' (115). While for many Marxist commentators this division in the worker became the locus of alienation and the myriad ills that accompanied that condition, for Berardi it is a separation and a distance in which the seeds of revolt could grow. It is also a separation that is now in the process of being overcome as the dogma of idiotism, in keeping with the latest marketing trend for all things holistic, wants us mind, body and soul. Under this regime, which supposedly represents the end of history, alienation takes a different form. In the immanence of commodity consumption and digitised communication we are separated from what is essential to us, namely the sense that something (anything) remains outstanding: that the future is still up for grabs.

To talk of this 'soul mining', to borrow a phrase from the musician Matt Johnson, is problematic because it seems to return us to a philosophical idealism, or to Christian doctrine of divinity. For Berardi, however, the soul is Spinozist, namely 'what the body can do' (2009:21), but for the purposes of the argument here the soul might also be understood in an Aristotelian sense, albeit slightly amended, where what he calls an 'ensouled thing' in Book II, chapter 2 of *De Anima* is described as both formal and material, meaning that the soul 'is the actuality of a certain kind of body' (414a 15–20). The soul is what makes a body *this* body. The soul is not a separate substance, but that which gives a shape to the body. What needs to be shown, then, is how the soul can inform our cultural practices, but also how it might be possible to take hold of the soul.

To understand this a little more it is necessary to adapt Aristotle's own application of his theory of the four causes to the problem of the soul. In Book II, chapter 4 of *De Anima* Aristotle presents the soul as 'the cause and first principle of the body' (415b 5–10). He then proceeds to qualify this by applying his theory of the four causes set out in Book 5 of his *Metaphysics*. The four causes are the material cause; the efficient cause; the formal cause; and the final cause. In Aristotle's texts it is important to remember that 'cause' translates the word *aition* (αἴτιον), which also means the reason for something, or that to which something is indebted. In his essay 'The Question Concerning Technology' Heidegger uses this four-fold conception of causality to talk about the creation of a chalice. The material cause is the silver the chalice is made from; the formal cause is the idea (*eidos*, form, look, aspect) of the chalice that gives the created thing its shape; the final cause is the ritual for which the chalice is used, a *telos* that can also be extended towards the community for whom the ritual is essential; while the efficient cause is the silversmith that crafts the object. The chalice is indebted to these four causes for its existence.

In *De Anima* Aristotle argues that the material cause is the body itself. Bodies have their physical limits and can only do certain things, but the soul should also be seen as that which motivates (efficient cause), gives shape (formal cause) and directs (final cause) the body. This means that for Aristotle the body is indebted to the soul in these three ways: it is effected or motivated by desire (*thymos*); it is formed through the advancement of the faculties of reason; and its goal is the pursuit of happiness. However, given that it has already been argued that our sense of self is not derived from some closed interiority but is part of the phenomenon of our being-in-the-world, the claim that these causes are internal to something called the subject is difficult to sustain. In terms of the formal cause we can say in line with Heidegger that it is essential to Dasein for its being to be an issue. It is essential for Dasein to find itself questioned, and it is this that gives Dasein its 'shape'. We can also say that Dasein is motivated by a desire to be at home, that is, to create a world that is meaningful, and in line with Hegel to have that meaning validated by others, by those we are with. We can also say that for Dasein what is at stake is its own future, the fact, as noted above, that Dasein always has something outstanding (Heidegger 1996:219). Importantly in all three of these causes to which the body is indebted to the soul it is evident that they have a quality we might ordinarily regard as cultural. Dasein's sense for its own freedom depends on the character of the culture in which it lives. In mythic or religious communities Dasein's freedom will be contained within specific cultural prescriptions pertaining to thought and action. Likewise, our desire necessarily passes through others and in this passage is directed to all manner of things that might claim to satisfy it. With regard to the final cause, what we aim at is also set in our relations with others and is projected from within an already shared set of meaningful practices. This was referred to in chapter 1 as Dasein's facticity. When considered in relation to Heidegger's critique of the self-subsistent subject the Aristotelian soul can be shown to have a significant degree of 'externality'. Efficient, formal and final causes are all mediated by our being-in-the-world. While the being of each singular Dasein is an issue for it, it is culture and the historical epoch in which we live that shapes, motivates and directs our questioning.

To think this interpretation of the soul specifically in relation to culture, it is also possible to map these causes onto Raymond

Williams's analysis in *The Long Revolution* (1965:57). While the body and its practical involvement with the world remains the material cause, Williams's notion of 'ideal' culture can be equated to the final cause, while his argument regarding 'documentary' culture, and in particular the role of the 'selective tradition' (67), can be taken to be the formal cause. This leaves Williams's idea of 'social' culture or the lived culture of everyday social interactions as the efficient cause. While Williams defines ideal culture as 'the best that has been thought and written in the world' (57), such ideals play a limited but not unimportant role today as either the cultural capital that supports hierarchies of social differentiation, or as the moral window dressing that gives military and economic assaults on the weak some credence of legitimacy. Other than that 'the best that has been thought' is now reduced to the single concept of the free market from which all other claims to goodness are now derived. This is idiotism's final cause. Likewise, the formal cause of the 'selective tradition' writes history as the natural progression towards the free market as the perfect system. Such a history is written from the perspective of power in the present in which everything that has passed gives support to the shape of our current culture as consumerist. This is why Thatcher could use the popular expression 'soul of the nation' and this is why neo-liberalism can go after it. A nation's culture is the extended soul that shapes each body, and shapes it according to a set of ideal and historical signifying practices. Change these practices and you change the soul, or rather you give it a different causal capacity to shape and focus bodies. Taking hold of the soul-culture has always been a problem though because where Williams believed the ideal and the documentary were related because a sense of each can be derived from extant resources (literary, artistic, philosophical, bureaucratic, etc.) the 'social' view of culture is not entirely recoverable as so much of the speech and action that makes up our everyday communication evaporates into thin air. However, Berardi's point is that with the advent of digital information technologies and the monitoring and archiving of everyday communication we have entered an age in which the unrecoverable aspect of the soul has simply become a problem of writing the best algorithm.

Neo-liberalism can thus take over all three of the non-material causes to set the finality (ideal), form (documentary) and motivation (social) that give bodies their actuality, that is, the historical character of their practical existence. Culture not only becomes a new resource for the production of value it becomes the ultimate disciplinary or framing device for the production of worlds. 'The soul, once wandering and unpredictable, must now follow functional paths in order to become compatible with the system of operative exchanges structuring the productive ensemble' (Berardi 2009:192). The soul wandered and was unpredictable precisely because it was in part radically undetermined. The efficient cause of lived culture might take place within a historically sedimented environment shaped by the formal and final causes of History and the Good, but these always remain contested precisely because the efficient cause of lived culture is where the meaning of a world is reproduced *and* contested through the multiform and myriad paths of everyday speech and action. For Berardi, however, it is precisely at this level of 'semiotic flux' that 'exploitation is exerted' (2009:22) under the current regime. Seen from a slightly different perspective, namely the distinction between 'work time' and what we might call 'free time' Christian Marazzi has argued that where automatism might be seen to have freed up work time this is only because under the post-Fordist conditions of the New Economy 'there has been an explosive increase in the linguistic-communicative-relational time of living labour, the time that [...] involves inter-subjective communication or value-creating cooperation' (2008:54). The New Economy functions as much through our 'free' communication on Facebook, for example, as it does through those operations required of us in our work time. In this way neo-liberalism exerts a form of cultural capture hitherto unknown. In the process the soul loses 'its tenderness and malleability' (Berardi 2009:192).

In the final chapter I will return to this issue to show why despite the dogmatic tendencies of idiotism it is not possible to petrify the soul, but for now it is important to address the appropriation of culture for the current regime of accumulation in order to show just how pervasive the dogma is. To do this it will be useful to make a few introductory remarks about what has come to be called consumer culture and the role the commodity plays in the mediation of social relations, but the aim here is to focus primarily on what Thatcher sought to engineer, namely the personalisation of culture. Under these conditions a very different understanding of publicness is emerging, one that is much closer to the publicity of promotion and advertising in which visibility and attention – 'mind-share' – is an end in itself. How the term public is understood is shifting from what Habermas described as an openness that doesn't necessarily mean 'general accessibility' (1992:1) to a generalised exposure that doesn't necessarily mean openness. Likewise, the public authority that

Habermas described as promoting 'the public or common welfare of its rightful members' (2) has now become an increasingly corporate authority promoting privatisation and individual self-interest as the only thing common to everyone, while the notion of public opinion as 'critical judge' (20), integral to his notion of the bourgeois public sphere, increasingly descends into the judgemental criticism in keeping with the now dominant model for the democratic process: the celebrity reality programme or talent show. In all of this the good is measured in the quantitative immanence of 'hits', 'likes', telephone-polls, and search-engine rankings.

CONSUMER CULTURE

In his excellent study entitled *Consumer Culture and Modernity* Don Slater explores the tension that has existed between 'culture as a critical social ideal' (1997:74) and consumption understood in relation to the baser instincts and appetites through which individual desire is permitted to 'triumph over abiding social values and obligations' (63). The notion of a consumer culture has, therefore, always been seen to be an oxymoron within conservative and elitist circles, suggesting that it must involve some very progressive possibilities (see Miller 2001). Yet, while an analysis of contemporary consumer culture will reveal all manner of resistances to the passivity and homogenisation assumed to be part of mass culture, my concern regarding the nature of idiotism remains the way that capitalism has come to increasingly extend itself across all forms of social life and it has done this primarily through the commodification of culture. Early studies of the phenomenon talk of commodities as symbolic goods, where what Baudrillard called 'sign value' superseded use value. Today, of course, commodities do all manner of cultural work or have added cultural value. Aside from the ubiquitous claims to display one's individuality, attitude, confidence and independence, the consumer is offered the chance to be revolutionary, ecological, ethical, charitable and fair without doing anything other than purchasing a product. The pervasive nature of promotions has also led William Leiss et al (2005) to speak of adverts as the new etiquette manuals offering a range of representations regarding manners, health, social expectations, and a range of public and private behaviours. In many respects, though, this is the continuation, albeit in exaggerated form, of the close link that has existed for a long time between social and cultural differentiation and the practices of consumption, namely the function of display and the use of products as markers of distinction. From this perspective consumption has always been socially and culturally important. Taking up Sekora's work on luxury (1977) Slater notes that the public reading of the sumptuary laws from church pulpits continued into the nineteenth century. In that world consumption beyond need, but more importantly beyond one's station was 'a form of sin, rebellion and insubordination against the proper order of the world, and represents moral, spiritual and political corruption, as well as a form of madness' (Slater 1997:69). The social disquiet recently caused when a section of the British working class, those pejoratively referred to as Chavs, adopted the Burberry brand as their signature clothing, indicates how sumptuary laws continue to operate and how what are deemed to be inappropriate displays of luxury remain forms of insubordination. No longer read from the pulpit but disseminated via the numerous screens of our electronic media, consumption beyond one's needs is encouraged in every walk of life, while the concept of station is simultaneously reinforced and undermined through the commercial etiquette manuals offering a range of aspirational lifestyles.

With regard to idiotism it is important that some awareness of these conflicts and resistances is maintained, but we must also not lose sight of the fact that this specific example, as with innumerable other expressions of agency within consumer culture continues to function within macro politico-economic structures organised to the benefit of a transnational capitalist class. Such 'resistances' remain another form of cultural capture or, put another way, capitalism has appropriated the subcultural style of appropriation. Where the Teddy Boys, Punks and Ravers can be shown to have taken over cultural objects and symbols and reused them in a manner that generated a significant amount of cultural friction, one of the critiques of consumer culture is that it incorporates a wide variety of subcultures that now seem to come pre-packaged. Because the dominant manifests itself as the simple injunction to consume, and because under the mature conditions of post-Fordism the New Economy is geared to cater for increasingly niche markets, sub-cultural expression is absorbed at an increasingly rapid pace. For cultural theorists such as Jim McGuigan this phenomenon requires us to speak of 'cool capitalism [...] defined by the incorporation, and thereby neutralisation, of cultural criticism and anti-capitalism into the theory and practice of capitalism itself' (2009:38). This is epitomised, he argues, by the incorporation of black music as 'the cultural face of such a capitalist embrace' (96), and especially those sub-genres emerging out of the socio-economic conditions of deprivation and exclusion that initially gave rise to hip-hop. 'Coolhunting' might still be done by hipsters but these are now the advance guard for the marketing executive and the investment analyst, integral members of the new 'creative class' whose function is to 'create meaningful new forms' (Richard Florida in McGuigan 2009:163).

This incorporation of the soul into the regimes of capitalist production has been central to critical thought since the publication of Herbert Marcuse's *Eros and Civilization* in 1955. At the time Marcuse was committed to showing how the erotic and libidinal life of each member of society – a life ordinarily central to creative and potentially liberatory practices – is drawn into capitalist production as the fuel that increases consumer demand. This idea is interesting, however, because it raises another central issue when addressing culture, namely its supposedly civilising effect, or culture as a counter to the state of nature. In Marcuse's version the potentially chaotic and destructive capacities of the life instinct or pleasure principle are (excessively) repressed by the civilising effect of the reality principle, something he renamed the performance principle or the stratification of an acquisitive and antagonistic society according to the competitive performances of its individuals. Interestingly, though – and this, of course, is the point of Marcuse's intervention – this seems to be little more than a *cultivation* of the state of nature rather than its replacement by the civilising effect of culture. Fifty years later such a condition becomes readily apparent. As Berardi notes, the culture of deregulation suggests an origination in the cultural avant-gardes 'heralding the end of every norm and constrictive rule' (2009:186), something that intimates a move in the direction of Marcuse's *eros*, and yet what deregulation actually instantiates is a condition where there is no longer any *contestation* concerning rules: 'The only legitimate rule is now the strictest, the most violent, the most cynical, the most irrational of all rules: the law of [the] economic jungle' (186). Deregulation is ultimately de-civilising because it frees 'economic dynamics from any tie' (188) other than its own. Liberals and neo-liberals alike have always argued that trade brings peace, but what capitalism really wants is the taming of the state of nature, its setting to work in and as a series of self-interested competitive performances, something crystallised, according to Gilles Deleuze, in the model of the corporation that 'constantly presents the brashest rivalry as a healthy form of emulation, an excellent motivational force that opposes individuals against one another and runs through each, dividing each within' (1992:5). According to this logic the cut-throat world of the TV reality show *The Apprentice* is the first variation of idiotism's ideal cultural form.

While these elements of consumer culture are crucial for the condition I have called idiotism where an increasing range of cultural practices and exchanges are mediated through the commodity form it is the personalisation of culture, the specific shaping of the soul that Thatcher sought to engineer, that I am most interested in. On this topic it was Richard Sennett who first addressed the threat to the idea of publicness posed by the pursuit of the personal. As noted above, we increasingly live in a culture that valorises exposure while undermining openness. We regularly disclose ourselves on social network sites – to the point where one user I recently encountered on Facebook had to be reminded that Facebook was not his therapist's office – while demonstrating little concern about what these sites do with the information we feed them. This linking of the idea of publicness to notions of intimacy, expression and personality is of the upmost importance. Thought in cultural terms, and certainly in relation to the dominant cultural forms of celebrity and the social network site, media intrusion in the case of celebrity, and media extrusion in the case of social networking would suggest a loss of privacy that doesn't chime with a condition defined by the increased valorisation of the private; but what is demanded by our increasingly mediatised and celebrity endorsed culture is that the private gives up its secret and is set to work through a continual flow of personal and intimate expression. In the end the important distinction between public and private is replaced by a notion of publicity based on exposure, disclosure, display and promotion that becomes an integral part of the post-Fordist shift towards 'soul mining'. At the level of culture the public and the private appear to have collapsed into one another.

PERSONALITY

In *The Fall of Public Man* Sennett expresses his concerns for a culture 'ruled by intimate feeling as a measure of the meaning of reality' (2002:326). When Sennett argues we need 'masks' (264) as a means of enabling engagements with others he is advocating a need for privacy that I would endorse: privacy as a necessary moment in the pursuit of non-private, genuinely public ends. Sennett is therefore not attempting to protect the political from the inevitability of partisan interests but from the dominance of charisma and the cult of personality that has come to define politics in the style dominated age of consumer capitalism. For when the market is everything, selling is everything, and politics becomes just another business in our densely mediated promotional culture. According to Sennett there has been a dramatic and destructive shift towards the personal (*idios*) and the intimate in political life. The central claim of Sennett's book is that in an age of charismatic display and commodified politics, privacy still has a role to play: 'people can be sociable', he writes (and by extension discharge the responsibilities of public office) 'only when they have some protection from each other' (2002:311). This is not a matter of stricter privacy laws for those in public life, but an argument in favour of roles and indeed role-playing that were originally understood to be means of social rather than self-expression. This is the very basis of civility in public life, for Sennett. It is through roles and the adoption of masks that we might come to understand how others feel and get a broader sense of a differentiated, but socially connected polity, or *demos*.

What Sennett was especially concerned about was how this loss of 'mutual distance' (311) also led to a focus on the actor instead of the action and the 'working out in terms of personal feelings public matters' (5). What characterises modern politics in the age of the mass media, according to Sennett, is the idea that 'what makes an action good [...] is the character of those who engage in it, not the action itself' (11), and this has dire consequences for politics and for the accountability of those in public office. Sennett writes: 'The modern charismatic leader destroys any distance between his own sentiments and impulses and those of his audience, and so, focusing his followers on his motivations, deflects them from measuring him in terms of his acts' (265). For Sennett the problem for politics now is that 'what matters is not what you have done but how you feel about it' (263), and in recent times there has been no better example of this than Tony Blair, whose resignation speech in the style of the intimate confessional perfectly encapsulates this irresponsibility: 'I was, and remain,' he said, 'as a person and as a prime minister, an optimist. Politics may be the art of the possible; but at least in life, give the impossible a go. Hand on heart, I did what I thought was right. I may have been wrong, that's your call. But believe one thing, if nothing else. I did what I thought was right for our country'. Under these conditions, Sennett argues, leadership becomes 'a form of seduction' (265).

Today, politics is more about image than substance. This turn to personality and intimacy has been necessitated by the increased alignment of both left and right with free market doctrine, thereby leaving very little room for parties and candidates to set out what they stand for. In this situation the individuality of a politician's personality can make all the difference. As computers have rendered car design increasingly uniform, advertisers have had to make the most of small differences, or simply attach a whole range of signifiers quite arbitrarily to their product in order to make it distinct, and much the same happens in today's political circus. While the election of one particular politician can make what seems to be a world of difference – the shift from a Bush White House to an Obama White House, for example – it is also the case that a lot remains the same. As noted in chapter 1, given that the fundamental doxa regarding a formally democratic free market capitalism remains unquestioned no matter who is elected, we find ourselves in a situation where electing a government is little more than choosing between the presentational styles of different fund managers.

The loss of masks can also be seen in the world of work where labour increasingly takes on a more personal form whether by intention or compulsion. Ordinarily we take our jobs or occupations to be one role amongst others. For the majority of people work is just something to be done, a role that needs to be played while their sense of self is more closely tied to other roles as parent, lover, music or sports fan, collector, volunteer, friend and numerous other modes of being-with-others through which we might gain a greater sense of self. Because work is often nothing more than the exchange of labour in return for a wage, alienation is not simply the separation of the producer from what is produced, but must also be seen as a point of disjunction where bodies are actualised by causes understood in some sense to be alien. Compared to this, a distinctive feature of the current regime of accumulation that sets the 'soul to work' is one where job and occupation are increasingly seen to be integral to what Stanley Cohen and Laurie Taylor call 'identity work' (1992:40). In an age where capital operates increasingly through the absorption and deployment of those areas traditionally seen as cultural – narrative, language, art, image, taste, style, leisure – work is increasingly seen as an expression of personality. The point is not that alienation is overcome, it is more the case that an increasing number of workers see little disjunction in the causes that shape them and little distinction between some putative 'life' and their work.

For Berardi, where enterprise formerly meant 'invention and free will' (2009:77) and labour was taken to be a form of impersonal repetition these two processes are now 'less opposed in [both] social perception and in the cognitive workers' consciousness' (77). In support of this Berardi notes that during the 1980s and increasingly in the 1990s, precisely the decades when the new regime of accumulation emerged, 'average labour time increased impressively. In the year 1996, the average worker invested in it 148 more hours than their colleagues did in 1973' (78). This can obviously be explained by the broader cultural shifts that took place in the 1980s where the pursuit of economic wealth supplanted other definitions of the good life. For Berardi it was the decade that promoted 'a life model totally focused on the value of wealth, and the reduction of the concept of wealth to economic and purchasing power' (81). In such a world, time is projected according to the need to acquire and accumulate the power to consume, but consumption is also 'fast, guilty and neurotic [...] because we can't waste time; we need to get back to work' (82). Enjoyment is thereby supplanted by loss, but that loss is recoverable through labour, and it is recoverable not simply because work provides the purchasing power that offers us the possibility of 'identity work' through consumption, but because labour has increasingly taken on the guise of enterprise and therefore facilitates 'identity work' itself. According to Berardi it is important to understand a decisive factor: 'while industrial workers invested mechanical energies in their wage-earning services according to a depersonalized model of repetition, *high tech* workers invest their specific competences, their creative, innovative and communicative energies in the labor process; that is, the best part of their intellectual capacities. As a consequence, enterprise [...] tends to become the center towards which desire is focused, the object of an investment that is not only economical but also psychological' (78). A little later, he comes to the conclusion that in the regime of cognitive labour no desire 'seems to exist anymore outside the economic enterprise' (96). Of course, this is not to say that work is no longer a role. High tech workers are still performing roles that are ideological affected by the current regime of accumulation, but these are not necessarily perceived as roles, as something one does or must do. For many, according to Berardi, work is becoming the immanent expression of personality.

The difficulty for theories such as Berardi's is that while the current regime does indeed operate through increased levels of cultural capture, cognitive or immaterial labour tends to overlook the fact that the vast majority of jobs – certainly globally, but also in the so-called advanced capitalist countries – are still tedious and repetitive, not to say unrewarding. Having said that, this situation requires that we consider the current regime's soul mining from a slightly different angle. When this is done it will be shown that the result aimed at is not dissimilar to what is happening at the level of cognitive labour. In his wonderful account of the ever-more precarious nature of low-paid or unskilled work entitled *Non-Stop Inertia* Ivor Southwood offers a compelling, first-hand account of the 'commitment' now required from all those looking for work. Referring to the management and display of feelings and affect that Arlie Hochschild called 'emotional labour', Southwood argues that this has now 'extended far beyond the traditional spheres of sales or corporate hospitality' (2011:25), and that even in the more menial jobs it is deep rather than surface acting that is now expected. He describes his own experience of applying for a pre-Christmas shelf-stacking job in Asda (a UK subsidiary of Wal-Mart) and the multiple-choice personality questionnaire that he was asked to complete followed by a screening of a 'corporate documercial' after which the applicants were asked to design a poster based on the video that 'would "sell" Asda to a potential employee' (29). He continues: 'It might seem odd to approach retail recruitment from the point of view of promoting the company to its own staff, rather than to its customers; but then […] this process is not so much about "selling" in the old sense, but about instilling a particular way of performing-thinking-feeling; making the candidates claim this positive attitude as their own and recognise it in others, as something natural and almost spiritual, rather than artificially imposed' (29). This, then, goes beyond the role-as-mask that Sennett speaks about and entails a process of intimate identification. All of which is supported by a growing 'precarity' (15) where the 'precariat' (16), made up of a vast pool of seasonal, temporary, 'self-employed' agency workers, are under mounting pressure to conform with this soul mining due to the volatility, unpredictability and general instability of work in which risk is increasingly passed from corporations to employees (or 'jobseekers'). From the 'cognoscenti' to the 'precariat', and across all other strata of the new regime's labour force, the expression of intimacy and personality in work means that work and life are becoming increasingly blurred. Another feature of idiotism, then, is that the life that was not work, those cultural practices that remained to some degree outside albeit still in relation to the world of work, have been gradually colonised by it.

To return to Sennett's thesis, he argues that the rise of personality and intimacy can be understood as 'the erosion of a sense of self-distance' (267) that is the cornerstone of public civility. As we saw with Berardi's concerns about cognitive labour, because it is communicative, symbolic and affective it 'belongs more essentially to human beings: productive activity is not undertaken in view of the physical transformation of matter but communication, the creation of mental states, of feelings and imagination' (84). Likewise, Southwood clearly documents this loss of self-distance as manual and casual workers are increasingly asked to fully identify with the work they do in the new 'jobseeker' culture. For Sennett, however, the key activity is play. By this he does not mean the immersive, self-expressive activity that play is sometimes associated with, the sort of play that adults partake in when they are 'letting off steam' or 'getting in touch with themselves'. It is rather the serious play of children in which they experiment with roles, rules and perspectives, and is largely predicated on exchange, exploration and the projection of alternative worlds. Play is therefore essential for self-distance and for the civility that it encourages. Loss of such play can be socially catastrophic: 'To lose the ability to play is to lose the sense that worldly conditions are plastic. This ability to play with social life depends on the existence of a dimension of society which stands apart from, at a distance from, intimate desire, need, and identity' (267).

The problem is that separation is seen to be bad. Sennett notes how self-distance is often seen negatively as a form of inauthenticity or alienation. There is a compulsion within our consumer culture for all things authentic, from food to tourism, from pop music to computer gaming, they all present themselves as paths to authenticity and the experience of the real. Commodities continually beckon us towards either genuine self-expression or authentic experience. In fact it is difficult to consume anything these days without having the 'experience' tied to it. This is not, of course, experience understood as the taste sensation that accompanies the necessary act of eating, for example, but a fully holistic, affective encounter aimed at our souls. For Berardi, the ubiquity and fleeting nature of such objects of desire represents 'the essential character of the pathologies of our time' (2009:172). Hyper-expressivity replaces repression, and what one must express is authenticity and personality. Let it out. Declare it. Be free. But in the context of Berardi's work, as was noted above, it is precisely the self-distancing of alienation that grounds a demand for something else, as does Heidegger's argument for Dasein's *existence*, where the '*ex*' signifies Dasein's being-out-side-of-itself, that is, a being for whom its being is an issue. For Heidegger, the issue of authenticity is tied explicitly to the projection of a different future, of not remaining caught up in the world as it already presents itself to us; to not be absorbed, an issue I will return to below. Here, the point that needs to be made is Sennett's when he remarks 'what gets lost in this celebration [of the personal] is the idea that people grow only by processes of encountering the unknown [and that] unfamiliar terrain serves a positive function in the life of a human being' (2002:295). When Sennett speaks of separation, then, it is precisely in a manner that counters the separation of the *idios* as self-enclosure. The separation involved in self-distancing effectively leaves something on the outside, or it is the opening of oneself to that which remains external and as yet undetermined. It works against what he calls the 'love of the ghetto' that negates 'the ability to call the established conditions of life into question' (295). Sennett names this condition narcissism or secular charisma. As opposed to the original form of religious charisma where a priest is said to be charismatic because at key points in a ritual he is understood to be momentarily visited by something transcendent and divine, secular charisma 'is rational; it is a rational way to think about politics in a culture ruled by belief in the immediate, the immanent, the empirical, and rejecting as hypothetical, mystical, or "premodern" belief in that which cannot be directly experienced' (276).

PUBLICITY

Moving on to the specific issue of the new form of publicity that has manifested itself in this personalisation of culture a few closing remarks on Sennett's rather out-dated attitude towards the media is required as the new forms of digital media have become the primary vehicle for the personalisation of culture. In the first instance it should be noted that Sennett's claim that 'electronic media embody the paradox of an empty public domain [...] the paradox of isolation and visibility' (283) still rings true, and is a key component in how publicity currently needs to be understood. While we talk of our new media age as being one of connectivity, writers such as Sherry Turkle (1995 and 2011) have moved a long way from their earlier enthusiasm regarding digital technologies to a much more sceptical view as to the benefits that such machines offer. Having said this, the early optimism of her book *Life on the Screen* was not mistaken, she was simply researching in a cultural environment in which the latest media developments, especially those that were internet or web-based, did indeed offer lots of reasons to be optimistic. Her most recent work, significantly entitled *Alone Together*, is much closer to Sennett's concerns about isolation and visibility simply because the political, economic and technological environment in which our media machines currently operate and in which Turkle is now researching has radically changed. While Sennett's observation that communications technology is geared towards 'openness of expression' (262) and the overcoming of barriers to that expression could easily be read as a contemporary description of online social networking, there are elements of his analysis regarding the production of passivity and silence in a mass audience that assumes uni-directional, mass media technologies that have long been supplanted by differentiation, interactivity, feedback, and the 'dial-up' approach to media consumption. In the current technological environment of ubiquitous media and ubiquitous computing the argument that media instigate 'complete repression of audience response' (284) is no longer supportable, if indeed it ever was. In many respects Sennett takes an attitude towards the media that the then new discipline of Cultural Studies, emerging at the time in Britain, was trying to challenge. Against the perceived pessimism of German (Frankfurt) Critical Theory and French Structuralism, which seemed to offer little escape from the culture industry or the conditioning of ideology, British Cultural Studies was on the lookout for examples of agency and resistance in popular culture that kept *historical* materialism very much alive. These documents of resistance for which the Birmingham Centre for Contemporary Cultural Studies (CCCS) earned an international reputation were nevertheless framed within arguments in political economy that never lost sight of the nature of power. Unfortunately, while this search for popular forms of resistance took Cultural Studies down the important route of seeking out and documenting alternative media audiences and active forms of consumption, much of what passes as Cultural Studies has lost sight of the macro issues in political economy that had informed earlier understandings of power relations. With the break-up of CCCS by Birmingham University the acronym now belongs to the Consumer Credit Counselling Service, which, in a world once high on consumption but now depressed by the weight of debt, seems wholly appropriate.

In this area Jodi Dean is again helpful not only because she continues important work in the tradition of Cultural Studies, which ensures the study of agency is always set against the functioning of ideology, but also because her work on the new media regularly returns to the issue of publicity. While Jodi Dean is pessimistic about the progressive potential of new media, she is nevertheless prepared to 'wager' (2009:173) that we can break out of the ideological deadlock that currently captivates us, but to do this we need to understand the extent of that captivation and how new media technologies are becoming increasingly complicit with it. In the early years of humanities research into digital culture there was a general optimism regarding the possibilities afforded by these new networked forms of communication that suggested decentralisation, a resistance to hierarchy, and alternative perspectives on the supposed objective state of affairs. Much, then, was written about the potentially liberatory role of the internet and cyberspace. For Dean, however, this failed to understand this new form of communication in relation to the global flows of capital. Indeed the shift to the post-Fordist model of flexibility and mobility sat very well with the circulation of communication across the internet leading Dean to coin the phrase 'communicative capitalism' (2002). While many commentators believe an increase in circulation of information to be a positive thing Dean points out it is in fact a problem for those wishing to affect cultural and political change because in the age of circulation criticism 'doesn't stick as criticism. It functions as just another opinion offered into the media-stream' (2009:21). While the abundance of messages is supposed to be an index of democratic potential, under communicative capitalism messages simply become 'contributions to circulating content – not actions to elicit responses. The exchange value of messages overtakes their use value' (26). She goes on to argue that in this situation the nature or quality of the contribution 'remains secondary to the fact of circulation' (26).

Given this, the optimism of early digital culture, for Dean, was in fact just another manifestation of the 'technological fetish [that] covers over and sustains a lack' (2009:37). Such a fetish arises in a society haunted by a response to technology that is at once phobic and messianic. What Dean offers is not so much a technophobia, as it is not technology *per se* that is the problem, but a scepticism based on an understanding of how socio-economic conditions have shaped technology. Failing to take into account those conditions is what leads to the adoption of the fetish where technology does the doing for us, and acting through it ensures we 'remain politically passive' (38). The problem with early approaches to digital communication, according to Dean, was the idea that the 'political purchase' of the technology was taken as a given: 'A website *is* political. Blogging *is* political' (41). There is an immediacy here that chimes with Sennett's notion of secular charisma, although here it is of a technological order: the immediate act of communication is sufficient. The fetish is thus also a form of condensation in which the whole complex of political life is reduced 'to one thing, one problem to be solved and one technological solution' (38).

This surfeit of information has also compounded a problem that Dean had highlighted earlier, namely that 'technoculture materializes the belief that the key to democracy can be found in uncovering secrets' (2002:44). In such a situation democracy is reduced to the 'compulsion to disclose and the drive to surveil' (45); 'revealing, outing, and uncovering' (46) become the principles of a democratic polity. Again, this is the manifestation of Sennett's concerns regarding intimacy where perceived misdemeanors in a politician's private life have greater significance than falsifying intelligence in order to take a country to war. There is also a problem whereby the quantity and speed of information continually makes us always feel uninformed, which encourages the demand for more, in a never-ending cycle of crisis: an informational panic-democracy where the need to know effaces any consideration of what it is that we ought to find out. Here, Dean argues, 'democratic governance becomes indistinguishable from the intensifications and extensions in the circulation of information' (151), and importantly its role in and as the market is disavowed (159). E-democracy, and by extension now the traditional modes of democratic governance, are nothing more than a problem of 'access' (15). Good government is the creation of ever more web sites containing terrabytes of information that produces an instant snow-blindness should you try to go anywhere near it. Access becomes its own opacity, knowledge is reduced to information retrieval, and disclosure morphs into concealment.

The cultural icon for this condition of publicity as exposure is the celebrity, now celebrated for nothing beyond the immediate fact of having made themselves more visible than other people. Where celebrity was formerly attached to some feat or achievement the majority of today's celebrities are examples of the secular charisma that makes people famous for being famous. Visibility and exposure assume a new social status, while reading 'revelations' about their lives or getting to know their 'secrets' becomes the power of the powerless. This is the peculiar dance played between secrecy and publicity that Dean is primarily concerned with. For her, it is this type of 'openness' that makes 'democracy' 'functional as technocultural ideology' (2002:162). In other words, from the pages of the broadsheets to the glossy covers of celebrity magazines democratic process becomes more and more aligned with presentation and revelation. In December 2009 it was widely reported that Simon Cowell, the man who re-invented the talent show by feeding it steroids, thereby giving us X-Factor, floated the idea of a 'political X-Factor' in which politicians could present ideas on a live show and voters could choose those they preferred. A key feature would be a red telephone that would light up if the Prime Minister wanted to intervene – something that, conscious or not, Cowell had presumably picked up from the camp Batman TV series of the 1960s. It is easy to see why people would baulk at the idea that this conveyor belt for celebrities with the life-cycle of disposable razors could have anything to do with democratic government, but doesn't it represent a Baudrillard-style logic of excess? Isn't our promo-panic-democracy destined to implode under the density of its own publicity?

This reduction of publicness to publicity is nowhere more in evidence than in the relatively recent phenomenon of web-based social networking sites. While it is important not to lose sight of the fact that these new media forms that splice together the global and the personal certainly carry important political potential, Facebook, Twitter and Tumblr, amongst others, reflect the increasing tendency towards publicity as exposure. To have no presence on Facebook or Twitter is simply to have no presence. In an age of growing surveillance we seem to be internalising the phenomenon and wilfully making ourselves as visible as possible. This culture of information dovetails all too easily with a culture of observing, tracking, collating and monitoring. This is the general accessibility without openness that has replaced the openness without general accessibility. For Dean, 'without publicity, the subject of technoculture doesn't know if it exists at all. It has no way of establishing that it has a place within the general sociosymbolic order of things, that it is recognized' (2002:114). To register as a subject 'one has to present oneself as an object for everyone else' (125). Unfortunately, while these seem to be outward-facing technologies that should encourage the sort of encounters with the unknown that Sennett sees as so important, latest research in the personalisation of computing, which I will turn to shortly, suggests otherwise.

MOBILE PRIVATISATION

Since at least the invention and popular take-up of the motor car cultural commentators have become increasingly concerned about the atomisation of public spaces. Writing about the car in connection to the rise of both suburbia and television Raymond Williams was one of the first people to voice concerns about the emerging culture of 'mobile privatisation' (1974:26). This was returned to in the 1980s with the advent of the Sony Walkman, which represented not only new forms of private consumption in public spaces, but the very alignment of that space to the mood of the user. For Michael Bull the device permitted the 'management of cognitive contingency' (2000:43), and aided the individual in their traversing of spaces not entirely in their control. Now, thanks to media convergence we have film, TV, music, telephone, text and social networking all in the one device known as the smart phone. Not only does this represent advancement in the privatisation of public space through uses of augmented reality – applications that superimpose requested information of a chosen public place over the material location when viewed through the phone's built in screen – they are also the machine that turns each and every one of us, irrespective of our jobs, into the cognitive labourers upon which the New Economy depends. Berardi writes:

> Global labor is the endless recombination of a myriad of fragments that produce, elaborate, distribute and decode signs and informational units of all sorts. Labor is the cellular activity where the network activates an endless recombination. Cellular phones are the instruments making this recombination possible. Every info-worker has the capacity to elaborate a specific semiotic segment that must meet and match innumerable other semiotic fragments in order to compose the frame of a combinatory entity that is info-commodity, Semiocapital. (89)

The point is that everyone who uses a smart phone is an info-worker (even stupid phones have enough intelligence to pass information of some kind into the system). Another way to speak of this is crowd-source capitalism. It goes without saying that the exploitation of labour has always meant that capitalism was crowd-sourced, the point here is that the crowd is no longer space-time dependent. It needs neither location nor duration. The crowd is an ever-modulating swarm. Where the 'Toyota model' represented the first phase of post-Fordism, the 'new organic composition of capital' (Marazzi 2010:56) is the 'Google model'. Just as Ikea 'delegated to the client a whole series of functions' (52), so the 'Google model' continuously draws consumers into the production of value; and it is for these reasons that scepticism towards the new publicity is warranted, not because it encourages misplaced outpourings of intimacy, but because the macro socio-economic conditions that underpin these new technologies necessitate the increased personalisation of a supposedly outward-looking, information-hungry, networked culture.

With such a surfeit of communication, impact is predicated on sensation, spectacle and novelty. This, however, is no simple accident or side-effect. According to Berardi, it is important to remember that when productive life becomes cognitive labour capitalism's soul mining means 'the constant mobilization of attention is essential to the productive function' (2009:107). In line with Dean's argument about circulation subsuming content, Berardi goes on to stress that what he calls the 'infocratic regime of Semiocapital founds its power on overloading' (183), proliferating a cultural white noise, and a 'hyper-stimulation of attention' that 'reduces the capacity for critical sequential interpretation, but also the time available for the emotional elaboration of the other' (183). Here the abundance of information directly impacts on the nature of the response. This is a problem also addressed by Marazzi who highlights what he calls a 'crisis of disproportion' (2008:67) in post-Fordist culture where attention in an age of increasing information 'has *diminishing* returns [...] It is a *scarce* and extremely *perishable good*'(66). He continues by quoting the economist Herbert Simon who noted that 'a wealth of information creates a poverty of attention' (66). An economy functioning through an ever increasing amount of information demands an increase in attention, and yet increase in the former *directly* decreases the latter. There is only so much we can attend to. This effectively becomes a new limit to capital and introduces a couple of very significant structural problems that Marazzi likens to those normally associated with the business cycle understood as imbalances in production and consumption. For Marazzi problems with the business cycle not only now arise as disproportion between information and attention but also in the tension between the material and the immaterial aspects of the economy. In the first instance, the amount of time dedicated to work in order to secure material consumption (including the material technologies that deliver information) eats into the 'free time' needed to secure attention, and, secondly, the increased destabilisation that accompanies the New Economy's assault on the Welfare State 'exacerbates the attention deficit of worker-consumers by forcing them to devote more attention to the search for work than to the consumption of intangible goods and services' (141).

This crisis generated through the disproportion of information to attention is leading to new developments in personalisation and personalised technology, and the smart phone, enabled with internet search engines, social networking and media streaming, has become the optimum tool in the struggle to negotiate its worst effects. Bringing together the best of both push and pull technologies and making these available at any time and in any place is one way in which properly free-time (time in which one might actually be permitted to be bored) is minimised in favour of attention-time. Given that attention is so valuable, it must not be allowed to be lost or allowed to 'drift off', but be captured for the informational matrix of communicative capitalism. To understand this we need to briefly return to the emergence of post-Fordism. As a new regime of accumulation the early manifestation that Marazzi calls the 'Toyota model' was predicated on just-in-time production and niche markets that responded to what consumers wanted. In the crowd-sourced, 'Google model' the distinction between production and consumption becomes blurred, but what still matters is *attending* to consumer 'need' and ensuring consumers *attend* to your claims to satisfying those needs. The effect has been to personalise the medium through which this two-way attention passes in order to maximise the relevance of information for each user. The revolution in computing, therefore, was not the development of the personal computer through which individuals might have greater access to the surfeit of information, the real revolution has been the personalisation of computer use where the surfeit of information is tailored to maximise 'hits' and 'likes'. In the early days of the internet when people spoke about the 'global village' and the resurgence of the counter-culture, Sherry Turkle's research presented users of MUDs as experimenters with different identities and practitioners of self-transformation (1995:260). Today, the personalisation of computing is demonstrating a trend towards something entirely different: not having oneself refigured through exposure to the outside world, but refiguring the outside world according to one's personal tastes.

While Dean uses the work of Albert-László Barabási (2003) to argue that the World Wide Web is divided into four major 'continents' creating hubs that have a certain gravitational pull on those moving through it and that movement from one continent to another is very rare, Eli Pariser, in his book *The Filter Bubble*, shows how computer personalisation via cookies and filters – the digital entities that remember our preferences, choices and current place within the information being used on websites – are increasingly closing down our access to anything beyond that which we have already designated as being worthy of our attention. Because attention is the most valuable commodity it is essential that companies know what we want so that they can target information at us that is more likely to be noticed. They also want to let others know, especially our 'friends' who are assumed to be like-minded, what has grabbed our attention. To this effect Facebook has recently introduced a practice known as 'frictionless sharing' whereby I no longer have to actively indicate I 'like' something, simply having attended to it (in any way) is enough to warrant it being automatically shared with all my Facebook 'friends'. The 'friction' that Facebook wants to get rid of is my judgement or decision-making which appears to be a hindrance to the free-flow of information in its pursuit of attention. This, of course, is all presented as a form of personal service, a digital digest of what others are in to and I am missing out on.

That personalisation can entail the circumvention of even our most basic critical capacities is troubling, but it is enabled by the digital robots invented to help us navigate the surfeit of information on the Web. According to Pariser, by using these computerised agents we are increasingly, and mostly unwittingly, drawing a boundary around the world of our immediate interests. He argues that the algorithms organising information according to preferences already indicated through click signals 'create a unique universe of information for each of us [...] which fundamentally alters the way we encounter ideas and information' (2011:9). The result is the digital shell that Pariser calls the filter bubble. It is invisible and we 'don't choose to enter' (10), but it is a 'cozy place, populated by our favourite people things and ideas' (12). He was motivated to research the problem when he became aware that Google would offer him different search results for the same search input dependent upon the computer he was using. The entrainment of the cookies on the different machines offered a view of the world based on the preferences of the most regular user. He also noticed how Facebook would effectively 'disappear' friends who weren't receiving what it perceived to be the requisite click signals to regard them as important. As Pariser explains: 'You may think you're the captain of your own destiny, but personalization can lead you down a road to a kind of informational determinism in which what you clicked on in the past determines what you see next [...]. You can get stuck in a static, ever-narrowing version of yourself – an endless you-loop' (16). He goes on to say that this produces 'a lot of bonding but very little bridging' (17). We still have access to more information than we know what to do with, but we are becoming less and less open to that which we don't already know. What is most troubling for Pariser, however, is that in the age of ubiquitous computing, when everything can be sprinkled with 'smart dust' and brought into the informational matrix, real world environments become organised according to the principles of the attention economy:

> The future of personalization – and of computing itself – is a strange amalgam of the real and the virtual. It's a future where our cities and our bedrooms and all of the spaces in between exhibit what researchers call 'ambient intelligence'. It's a future where our environments shift around us to suit our preferences and even our moods. And it's a future where advertisers will develop ever more powerful and reality-bending ways to make sure their products are seen.
>
> The days when the filter bubble disappears when we step away from our computers, in other words, are numbered. (192)

In this scenario, the smart phone becomes the ultimate means for cultural capture and the shaping of the soul deemed central to the neo-liberal project by one of its founding ideologues. And we need not think of this in conspiratorial terms; this is simply a structural phenomenon, the logical extension of an economic system constantly needing to open up new resources and new territories, both material and immaterial, in its pursuit of growth. In this way publicity becomes the heightened exposure to (and of) the personal, and the World Wide Web becomes my world-wide wants. This extended yet enclosed world is the central feature of idiotism as it is applied to the latest developments in digital culture.

No doubt futurists are already imagining embodied versions of this that operate through oral implants and lenses: for now, however, the smart phone remains the technological centre-piece of the attention economy. But this leads to one final concern that takes us back to the ontological problem set out in chapter 1, namely the tendency for Dasein to become absorbed in the world it already knows and lose sight of its potential for projecting alternative futures. This condition is especially acute at times of crisis (or boredom!). When one's usual habits and everyday routines are significantly disrupted a profound anxiety can arise in response to the groundlessness of things that can manifest itself on such occasions. To counter this Dasein has a tendency to busy itself, to throw itself into what it knows with extra vigour. Even where this busy-ness is not motivated by crisis Heidegger argues there is a tendency for Dasein to become '*entangled* in itself' (1996:166). This is an entanglement that is tempting because it is tranquilising, but unlike the tranquility we assume requires stillness Dasein's tranquility is a restlessness that drives it towards the perpetual hustle of everyday distractions.

The smart phone is the device that more than any other media technology instantiates this condition of tranquil busyness. To use a wonderful phrase coined by my former colleague Tracey Potts we are all 'app-happy' (Potts 2010). Constantly streaming information relevant to me whilst also deploying applications enabling the translation of my environment into any particular informational configuration that suits (what planes are actually flying over my head at this present time, the carrier, flight number and number of passengers, for example), I am in thrall to my seemingly unlimited knowledge. At no time is the smart-phone user left alone or left with nothing to do. The boredom that Heidegger (1995) believes is crucial to any reflection upon one's life is effectively prohibited. Code is law, and the code says you will be entertained. Immersed in what Heidgger calls 'idle talk' or what we should perhaps call the 'chat' that 'says what one is to have read and seen' (Heidegger 1996:161), as well as being driven by a curiosity that leaps from one novel piece of information to the next, the perpetual attachment to the smart phone exemplifies the busyness that Heidegger mockingly notes guarantees a 'genuinely "lively life"' (162).

While it might be essential for Dasein to project a future for itself, a future beyond the hustle of our 'always on' consumer culture, such projection requires some distance from it. However, by increasingly taking hold of the soul and its capacity to both shape bodies and determine practices, it is this distance that our personalised, always entertaining digital culture precisely obliterates in the immanence of information overload. Ultimately, this culture of access and exposure, of personality and intimacy is one in which our horizons are increasingly closed and circumscribed by forces ever more impersonal and distant. And this idea regarding the projection of a future introduces the issue that needs to be addressed in the final chapter. If the informational circulation of communicative capitalism tends towards a closed, autopoietic system that I have called idiotism, how does this relate to the hermeneutic condition that makes it essential for Dasein to question itself. Where communication increasingly works to reinforce one particular worldview and the power relations it sustains, can our hermeneutic condition still point to the possibility of alternatives?

6
Opening the World, or Democracy

Given the plethora of cheap consumer goods that direct our behaviour and the proliferation of entertainment that absorbs our attention it would not be difficult to argue that idiotism is a highly evolved and complex instance of the phenomenon Juvenal satirically referred to as *panem et circenses* (bread and circuses). We might even add that the accommodation of Juvenal's contemporaries into these circuses is another way in which the closure of the system is secured. As long as there are highly visible and extremely clever people satirising the dogma this gives credence to the belief that we still live in an open society. Just as we are told, all must be well in the house of democracy. While the bread and circuses analogy is pertinent it is nevertheless deeply problematic because of the stupefaction it assumes in those people supposedly caught up in the spectacle. This attitude is therefore also one that legitimises the power of the oligarchy who must rule because the majority are ultimately unable to know what is good for them. This is one of the central elements in what Jacques Rancière calls the 'hatred of democracy' (2006).

Against this, I have suggested that an ontological approach to ideology allows us to acknowledge that people can remain critical of the world 'as it is' while still carrying on with their lives in keeping with the references and assignments that organise it. What is more, in line with this analysis, our everyday practices remain the ground out of which new interpretations may yet arise. In other words, there is a fragility to our being-in-the-world that is neither the exclusive property of some privileged class who selflessly protect the stupefied from this 'dangerous truth', nor is it something the niche bread and circuses of post-Fordism can completely defend against. This also means that alternatives need not come about through a dramatic re-engagement with the world that only a political vanguard of heroic radicals is capable of achieving, they can also be effected through the fabric of everyone's mundane, quotidian practices. Despite the management of the entire social field in keeping with market imperatives and our enclosure within increasingly personalised social relations the essential questions regarding who we are and how we should live together cannot be put to rest. Our hermeneutic condition, that is, our ability to posit new interpretations cannot be permanently arrested no matter how much the ideologues would like to tell us history is over.

At one level this analysis remains deeply pessimistic because an ontological analysis accounts for how critical distance might still be accommodated within the world as it is, but it is also deeply optimistic because it argues that potential for change is immanent to even our most habitual of practices and that these are always susceptible to cracks. This means the task here is to explore the tension between democracy as a pacifier, where the formality of 'democratic' processes and institutions masks what is really a plutocracy in which a transnational capitalist class are permitted to do what they want, and democracy as the sign of a constituting power, no matter how weak it might appear to be, capable of producing profound rupture and the overturning of dogma. This use of ontology may well appear perverse given Heidegger's own distaste for all things democratic, and yet it is not necessary to read Heidegger entirely against the grain to be able to do this. His own conservative predilection for a special class of poets and thinkers able to live authentically should not hide the fact that Heidegger's work clearly shows how everyone has an interpretive relation to the world, and it is precisely this hermeneutic condition that enables us to have hope even in the midst of the deepest pessimism.

The total closure of idiotism as a dogmatic system will not end interpretation, as much as it might wish to. Idiotism's reduction of a plurality of worlds to a multiplicity of commodified life-styles will never suffice, and in a capitalist system that remains prone to crisis there will always be the opportunity for alternatives to emerge. It has also been noted that the dogma of idiotism took root not via explicit directives from the plutocrats (although it is the high priests of capital that most clearly benefit), but in the form of a common sense whereby it is simply 'obvious' that competition is an important social motor and that the free market is 'plainly' the best guarantee of freedom. However, as Gramsci argued, whilst still taking the form of a coherent worldview common sense is 'disjointed and episodic' (Gramsci 1971:324) and is another reason why the ideology shaping it is always susceptible to resistance. Ideas that have supposedly been swept aside by the new thinking can persist and even re-seed. This is precisely the case with all those terms like public, society, collective, and communal that idiotism disavows but clearly feeds off.

DEMOS

The problem for resistance, its first task, is to collect itself beneath a sign that speaks to a variety of actors trying to bring about change. As Simon Critchley notes, 'Politics is always about nomination. It is about naming a political subjectivity and organizing politically around that name' (2007:103). His own position is that such a name should not 'be articulated in relation to a pre-given socio-economic identity [...] but has to be aggregated from the various social struggles of the present' (91). For this reason, collective terms like 'the Proletariat' carry too much historical baggage for him and don't represent the particularities of struggles and claims that are currently being made around the globe. As David Harvey has pointed out, a significant by-product of the dispossession currently taking place under the auspices of idiotism's drive towards privatisation, deregulation and markets is different from the 'accumulation through the expansion of wage labour' (2005:178) that led more easily to the development of collective forms of resistance under the banner of labour. Current forms of dispossession fracture resistance by turning it into a version of identity or single issue politics. For Critchley, however, it is precisely these particular grievances that ought to be taken up as a sign for broader political projects, and cites the work Courtney Jung has done around 'the indigenous person' (108) as a name beneath which various political demands could come together.

Much like Hardt and Negri's appeal to the poor, the indigenous person or indigenous peoples do bring together a range of injustices that translate into wider issues and hint at new forms of solidarity, but I would like to argue that democracy, or rather *demos* (δημος), can still be the name under which 'the various social struggles of the present' can be collected and resistance to the dogma of idiotism mounted. The difficulty faced by this name is directly linked to the disrepute into which it has fallen. With the ascendency of idiotism, the supposed victory of the capitalist democracies has in reality more closely resembled the consolidation of plutocracy governed by an increasingly unaccountable oligarchy. We may vote for our politicians, but it is not our politicians that hold sway: it is increasingly the ratings agencies, banks and large transnational corporations that determine both domestic and foreign policy. Democracy has lost sight of its political essence and has been relegated to a social process that represents and satisfies expressions of preference within a clearly bounded set of options. According to this consensus, writes Rancière, 'our basic reality does not leave us the choice to interpret it and merely requires responses adapted to the circumstances, responses which are generally the same, whatever our opinions and aspirations' (2006:77). In the last few decades this consensus has been secured, as Rancière claims, by marrying the principle of wealth to the principle of science – or what we now know to be pseudo-science – 'in order to give oligarchy a renewed legitimacy' (78). It is only the quants and the trained economists who can have any real input into how society is to be directed, for they alone understand the levels of complexity involved and have the requisite knowledge and expertise for 'administering the local consequences of global historical necessity' (Rancière 2006:81).

The takeover in November 2011 by the technocrats in Italy perfectly encapsulates the current predicament. Aside from the sleight of hand that suggests politicians are not technocrats, i.e. not simply rolling out a given system across the globe, and that technocrats are not politicians, i.e. the global free market is not political, this situation signals something quite remarkable with regard to democracy, namely that the will of the people is an utter irrelevance. Just as the technopols stumbled upon the perfect enemy on 11 September 2001 when an open-ended, global war was announced against the concept of terror that could freely be attributed to any person of group using any kind of violence, so a new state of emergency seems to be taking shape following the collapse of the financial system in 2007–8 and the following sovereign debt crisis of 2011. The scale of the crisis created by the financial oligarchy and the technopols that support them seems to now give legitimacy to the complete bypassing of any democratic process whatsoever (a move that will increasingly be used in the future). As it has already been declared that the market is the very practice of democracy and that nothing else can be democratic, anything that is done to defend the market is a defence of democracy and no questions need be asked of the *demos*. The economic crisis has not only worked out in favour of the capitalist oligarchy, but it is so severe as to have brought about an undeclared state of emergency in which the laws pertaining to the election of a government can be suspended. Although Hardt and Negri did not couch their argument regarding the sovereignty of capital in Schmittian terms, the economic state of emergency quietly declared on 13 November 2011 with the appointment of Mario Monti as Italian Prime Minister certainly gives credence to such a claim. Importantly, the polemical heart has been carefully excised from the *demos* in the name of democracy. The *demos* no longer needs to be consulted because democracy is automatically in agreement with anything that is done for the sake of the market. Such is the consensus, and such is the challenge in taking *demos* as the name around which to gather and organise alternatives to idiotism. The pursuit of democracy is not the exclusive practice of liberals and therefore does not preclude the possibility of other forms of political organisation such as anarchism, socialism or communism. As I will show there is something deeply anarchic about the *demos*, and while its potential resistance to all forms of dogma will be addressed below, it is the more immediate counter to idiotism signified in the word *demos* that needs to be set out here. The initial and most direct way in which *demos* (δεμος) counters *idios* (ιδιος) is as its logical and linguistic opposite. In Greek where *idios* signifies the private the word *demos* means that which is common or public. This can mean something that is held in common, such as land, as revealed in the word δημεύω meaning to declare public property – and where δήμευσις would be the public confiscation that reverses the theft of common land through the system of private enclosure – or *demos* can refer to the public as a body of people. Here we also arrive at a very interesting feature of this word in that it deconstructs itself by signifying both the plebeians or common people, and the citizenry. In other words it is both those who are excluded from the political process and those who are central to it. This is because *demos* originally denoted a region or country district, and could also be used to refer to a township from where we derive the obscure English word deme, the sub-division of land that became the basis for political representation rather than the family of birth that had defined Greek aristocratic rule. Early democracy is thus based on residency rather than privilege. This link between the land and the *demos* also draws out another interesting meaning of the word as signified in the name Demeter (Δεμήτηρ), goddess of agriculture. Here *demos* has a strong connection to labour and to work, as well as to ecology and the environment. Buried deep inside the word democracy is this connection to the commons and to labour from which the current form of democracy as privatised consumer choice is very far removed.

This also leads to the second way in which *demos* deconstructs itself. When thought in terms of the citizenry it is integral to the *polis* understood as the city-state, yet thought in terms of the district or region it was originally understood to be the opposite of the *polis*. If we take the *polis* to simply represent the state – an identification that will need problematising below – then the *demos* has a peculiar relation to it in that it is both intimate yet foreign, integral yet separate. One reason why Critchley argues for a political name not based on a pre-given socio-economic identity is precisely because he is looking for something that cannot be easily appropriated by the state. 'True democracy', he writes, 'would be the enactment of cooperative alliances, aggregations of conviviality and affinity at the level of society that materially deform the state power that threatens to saturate them' (2007:117). What Critchley advocates, then, are forms of political association that create 'an *interstitial* distance' (113) within the state. The word *demos* signifies just that, and yet in the economic state of emergency recently declared we can begin to see the way in which capital is directly opposed to democracy, understood as more than the expression of preferences and the provision of privatised consumer choices. With capital having assumed the sovereign capacity for deciding on the state of exception, that is, when the agents of global capital take it upon themselves to suspend normal democratic procedures capital is no longer the friend of the *demos*, it has instead become the *démoboros basileus* (δέμοβορος ναςιλευς), the king that devours his people (Newman 1856:7) that Homer refers to in Book 1, line 231 of the *Iliad*. In this way all separation and any mark of distinction between *demos* and market/state is lost. When the people are consumed by capital and the entire social field is flooded by free market economics what passes as politics occurs in 'places that do not leave any space for the democratic invention of polemic' (Rancière 2006:82).

Chantal Mouffe (1993) has already shown us that when democracy becomes consensus it loses all meaning as the antagonisms democracy stages are buried beneath the dogma of generalised agreement. What I would like to explore, then, is the way in which *demos* if it is to mean anything must be understood in polemical terms. While the word offers possibly fruitful paths for the re-coupling of democracy with notions of the collective, the public and the commons, and with the related issues of labour and the environment provides numerous points for political mobilisation and fresh ways of thinking democratic socialism or communism, the primary aim here is not to set out an alternative model for socio-economic and hence political organisation, but to show how the polemical character of the *demos* registers hope for overcoming current (and future) dogma. In writing a book critical of dogmatic idiotism I am concerned not to revert to an alternative dogma by describing what is to be done. I am also mindful of not wishing to subscribe to the idea of 'a promised land', which is a phrase that mars David Harvey's otherwise brilliant book (2010:250). Against the closure of the current system the name *demos* signifies there is no end because as the setting in play of the parts and the divisions within the commons it is also without beginning. If there was a founding principle that ordered everything from the start there would be no need for the *polis* to open itself to the *demos* or for the *demos* to collect its parts in the *polis*: there would be no politics, just physics. If there is a founding principle it is a polemical one, the one that set democracy against aristocracy and must do so again. This polemical principle is, then, a matter of opening up the interpretation that has been closed off by the dogma of idiotism. To consider its specifically anarchic quality it will be necessary to take up Rancière's notion of a polemical democracy before returning to Heidegger's analysis to show how the *demos* is intrinsically tied to the overcoming of accepted ways of thinking and doing.

DEMOS AS DISAGREEMENT

In his various works on politics Jacques Rancière argues that despite the drift towards consensus politics is in fact based on a 'rationality of disagreement' (1999: xii). The nature of this disagreement also carries with it a disclosive element in that politics consists in the conflict 'over the existence of a common stage and over the existence and status of those present on it' (26–7). Politics is about the emergence and appearance of this or that party, group or class that had previously not been part of the established political order. In a process that Rancière calls 'subjectification' (35), politics 'makes visible what had no business being seen, and makes heard a discourse where once there was only place for noise' (30). Politics is thus the site of innumerable 'polemical situations' (56) where 'those who have no right to be counted as speaking beings make themselves of some account' (27). The polemical root of politics is thus the confrontation and 'contradiction of two worlds in a single world' (27), and if 'subjectification' is the process Rancière gives to a new distribution of who counts and who doesn't, 'identification' (36) is the process that seeks to maintain the already described or permitted distribution. This is also what Rancière calls the 'police' function and is understood by him as the 'allocation of ways of doing, [...] being, [...] saying' (29) and the assignment of each subject to its place and task. Under the dogmatic conditions of idiotism this police function is especially pronounced not only in relation to the closing off of alternative interpretations of how we should live together, but also in the way that those who suffer most from the current mode of economic organisation are rendered invisible by outsourcing or exporting the working conditions that we no longer deem acceptable. In this configuration politics is fundamentally 'antagonistic to policing' because it breaks with the given configuration of parts and 'divisions of the police order' (30). This is also not an occasional problem where confrontations only sporadically take place, but happens all the time because in Rancière's view politics 'runs up against the police everywhere' (32).

The second characteristic of politics for Rancière is that it pertains to equality and thereby carries out the 'original split in the "nature" of politics' (70). Here this means the division between those who count and those who don't is perpetually challenged through the pursuit of equality that is essential to the process of subjectification. More specifically it is a challenge to 'the order of kinship' (2006:45) and inclusion (or exclusion) according to birth that defined Greek aristocracy. However, what is interesting for Rancière is that this challenge is not altogether 'external' to the aristocratic system but a 'supplementary title' (47), or 'title of exception' (49) that resides within it. In the third book of Plato's *Laws* Rancière notes the seven titles that ensure good government. Of the seven, four relate to birth (parents, the old, masters – the highborn); two to nature (the strongest, those who know – the best); and a seventh title that is not actually a title, but is the most just: the 'favour of heaven and fortune'. This element of chance is a scandalous title that refutes all classification, and yet because Plato was suspicious of those who actively sought power, chance was deemed to be a very important element in the attempt to guard against tyranny. Here the drawing of lots is viewed as a key element for protecting against those able to take power through cunning, or the professional politicians who take power because they desire it, as is so prevalent today. The preservation of good government thus means that democracy is dependent on something defined as 'the very absence of every title to govern' (41), and that government needs this 'power of anyone at all' (49).

These two concepts of subjectification and equality, or the inclusion of anyone at all, are the two conditions that define politics as opposed to the police function that works to maintain an exclusive identity. For Rancière politics is the disjoining of government from what is perceived to be the natural difference contained in the title *aristos*, best. It is opposed to all forms of paternity – which would include the paternity of the market and its technopols – and the reduction of the public sphere to the rule of those already entitled and who wish to make it their 'own private affair' (55). Democracy is therefore the 'struggle against this privatization' (55) in favour of the universality of that title without title. According to Rancière democracy must 'constantly bring the universal into play in a polemical form' (62). To resist this, government by title continually represents equality as catastrophic for democratic civilisation: as the anarchic, excessive 'disorder of passions' (6). What I am seeking to present under the name *demos*, then, is precisely this polemical disruption to the accepted ways of thinking and doing that Rancière calls politics. I would also concur with the idea that democracy cannot be reduced to the state, and that 'wherever the part of those who have no part is inscribed' there is the *kratos* of the people (Rancière 1999:88).

The *demos* is thus this differentiation of the people from itself that emerges through new or reinterpretations of how we should live together. As Rancière argues: 'Democracy [...] is not a set of institutions or one kind of regime among others but a way for politics to be. [...] Democracy is more precisely the name of a singular disruption of [the] order of distribution of bodies' (99). In other words, there is democracy where groups 'displace identities as far as parts of the state or of society go' (100). It is therefore 'the institution of politics itself' (101). To understand democracy in this way it is necessary to interrogate a little more the idea that it is a particular way 'for politics to be', which requires further consideration of the relationship between ontology, the *polis* and the *demos*. It also demands a rethink of *polemos* understood as the dualism of police and politics. There is a danger that a politics that sees itself entirely opposed to the police function has insufficient understanding of how the disruption that defines politics will in turn seek to police and hence preserve its own emergence – that moment when subjectification becomes identification. To some extent Rancière's analysis remains too focused on the negating capacity of those parties giving an account of themselves in the attempt to secure a space on the stage. While this is absolutely crucial to politics, and politics cannot be thought without it, *demos* – as I am using it here – signifies a polemical condition that first *gives rise* to this negating action, and to address this more primordial *polemos* and see how it is at once political *and* policing in Rancière's sense we need to return to the work of Heidegger.

HEIDEGGER AND POLEMOS

Heidegger's reading of the Greek word *polemos* is taken from the Heraclitus fragment (numbered 53 in the standard Diels and Kranz edition) that reads as follows: 'War [*polemos*] is father of all, and king of all. He renders some gods, others men; he makes some slaves, others free' (Robinson 1987:37). The key for Heidegger is that *polemos* is both father and king; it is generative and governing or ruling; productive and preserving. It can therefore be said to contain both political and police functions in Rancière's sense. On such a reading *polemos* is not simply a violent struggle of becoming between already existing beings, but the principle that permits the very possibility of one being standing against, alongside, and even *with* another. This is why Heidegger interprets the fragment in the following way:

> The *polemos* named here is a conflict that prevailed prior to everything divine and human, not a war in the human sense. This conflict, as Heraclitus thought it, first caused the realm of being to separate into opposites; it first gave rise to position and order and rank. In such separation cleavages, intervals, distances, and joints opened. In the conflict a world comes into being. (Conflict does not split, much less destroy unity, it is a binding-together, *logos*. *Polemos* and *logos* are the same.) (1959:62)

The importance of this concept for Heidegger has been set out in Gregory Fried's (2000) excellent study in which he shows that such a *polemos* is essential to Dasein as the being for whom its being is an issue. This very question(ing) that is the essence of Dasein is the source of all human polemic. Every debate, contest, argument, disagreement, and conversely every joint venture has its root here. This is because the *essence* of Dasein lies in its *existence*, characteristics of which are not properties but 'possible ways for it to be' (Heidegger 1996:40). These characteristics therefore arise not from any positive attribute be that Platonic *thymos* or Nietzschean will, but from a freedom conceived in terms of being in the open, or, as Heidegger puts it, being held out into the nothing. Our freedom arises precisely from the lack of any ultimate ground and it is the nihilative moment of the nothing that is the root of all negating action. The nothing perpetually becomes manifest in those varied experiences of meaninglessness or groundlessness (loss of reason, cause, purpose, sense, relevance) when our world seems to slip away.

As Heidegger argued in the 1929 essay 'What is Metaphysics?':
'Only because the nothing is manifest in the ground of Dasein
can the total strangeness of beings overwhelm us. Only when the
strangeness of beings oppresses us does it arouse and evoke wonder.
Only on the ground of wonder – the manifestness of the nothing
– does the "why?" loom before us' (1998:95). In this sense the
questioning does not come from us, so to speak, but arises out
of the lack of any ultimate ground. This means that no answer to
the question can or should ever be taken as an adequate response,
which is what all dogma seeks to do. No answer can ever satisfy
or be co-terminus with a supposed human nature because what
is 'natural' to Dasein is to be held out into the nothing. This is a
condition that demands continuous interpretation and reinterpreta-
tion of the world in which we live. While Heidegger's conservatism
tends him to overplay the role of 'authenticity' with its suggestion
of the individual breaking from the herd, this interpretive practice
is always done with others because Dasein experiences itself as
'thrown projection' – born into a world of shared, culturally
sedimented references from which it must project a future. It is
this to which we can apply Fried's translation of *polemos* as an
'interpretive confrontation' (2000:31) with the world *as* it is given.
This interpretation, of course, should not be taken as a theoretical
meditation from a position of detachment, but something emerging
from our involvement with the world, which is always already
practical. Interpretation is therefore much closer to practice than
it is to theory.

In a book whose central thesis is germane to the argument here
Gianni Vattimo and Santiago Zabala argue that the shape of the
current *polemos* is precisely an attack on all interpretation in
the name of truth, and the truth of the free market in particular.
Hermeneutics has been displaced by a 'politics of description' where
the market is the true expression of human organisation and the
possessive individual is the true characterisation of human desire. In
this way the politics of description is 'functional for the continued
existence of a society of dominion' (2011:12), which is secured by
denying the laws of economics, for example, are 'historical products
put to work by some class, dominating group, or institutional-
ized establishment' (114). This is a situation that leads Vattimo
and Zabala to conclude that 'violence is the political meaning
of truth' (18), that truth claims attempt to fix the status of some
particular referent and in this enhance a particular centre of power
against alternative interpretations. Given this Vattimo and Zabala

argue that hermeneutics automatically takes a political stance as 'the thought of the weak' (2011:2). By the very fact that it seeks to re-open the possibility for an interpretive engagement with the world, hermeneutics is 'opposed to the objective state of affairs' (6) that those who have dominion are keen to police. In keeping with Rancière's argument for the politics of equality, what they call 'hermeneutic communism' counters the deployment of truth by re-opening the interpretive stage to all parties. This leads them to declare '*the end of truth is the beginning of democracy*' (23).

However, we do not need to divorce democracy entirely from the conception of truth. It is far better to develop a conflictual understanding of truth that can allow democracy to escape the constraints currently framing it, which is precisely what Heidegger's understanding of *polemos* allows us to do. While his early translation involved the use of the German word *kampf* (struggle) he gradually replaced this usage after 1933 with the German word *Auseinandersetzung* from which Fried develops the idea of *polemos* as interpretive confrontation. In German this word has many meanings including to separate, to set out, to explain, to talk or converse, and to argue. It is therefore very much in keeping with Rancière's conception of politics as disagreement. But Heidegger also uses it to invoke the positing, placing, exposing, founding or establishing (*setzen*) of particular differentiated beings (*auseinander*) in line with his translation of the Heraclitus fragment. While everyday German suggests *auseinandersetzung* is an argument or conversation more in keeping with the form of a dialogue, Heidegger uses it precisely for the setting in opposition that is the key to understanding Heidegger's life-long commitment to recovering a conflictual or polemical understanding of truth as 'Being-uncovering' (1962:262). Such an understanding stems from his reading of the Greek word for truth, *alētheia* (αλήθεια), which literally means without hiddenness, without forgetting, or from out of oblivion (*lēthe*). Heidegger translates *alētheia* and thereby understands truth as unconcealment. It is not a correspondence to an object that is deemed to already exist but the bringing-forth or presencing of an entity. This is, of course, closely related to a sense of practice or, in Heidegger's language, how we involve ourselves with the things around us. His famous example is of the different ways in which a poet and an engineer approach a river. One reveals it as a metaphor for human journeying while the other reveals it as a source of potential energy. What we take to be our world is an interpretation that already reveals beings *as* this or *as* that. Under idiotism the interpretation that holds sway (precisely by denying it is an interpretation) operates by viewing everything as the potential for the extraction of surplus value and remains oblivious to anything that doesn't. This means the world is not something external and permanent but something (continuously) disclosed, or brought into being in and through Dasein's interpretive practices.

Truth as this 'being-uncovering' is a two-fold struggle. Firstly, there is the struggle just alluded to whereby Dasein experiences itself as 'already in a definite world' dominated by the most general interpretation (Heidegger 1996:203). However, because the world is neither natural nor God-given the lack of any ultimate foundation or appeal to finality always means that conflict and contestation are immanent to even the most dominant ideologies. There is always potential for things to be revealed in a different way, especially during times of crisis. While Heidegger tends to reserve the term 'public' for those instances of everyday life where this polemical character of the world is hidden, if we are to move beyond the residual individualism that haunts Heidegger's assessment of authenticity it is important to argue that what is properly public or what is proper to the *demos* is the securing of places for this conflict of interpretations to take place, and it goes without saying that such spaces need to be independent of all commercial communication and what Rancière calls 'the monopoly of [...] expert government' (2006:83).

The second way in which Heidegger understands truth as polemical is through an analysis of the differentiation within the realm of Being itself whereby Being is not reducible to the beings that have already been brought to light through our interpretive practices. Truth must therefore be understood in terms of both disclosure and withdrawal. For everything that appears to us something remains hidden, but philosophy, for Heidegger, forgets this differentiation. In the lecture series entitled *Parmenides* Heidegger argues that in the movement from *alētheia* through the various Latin translations of *veritas*, *adequatio*, *rectitude*, and finally the modern *certitudo* 'the conflict indigenous to the very essence of truth' (1992:18) has been lost. He goes on to say: 'For us, "truth" means the opposite: that which is beyond all conflict and therefore must be nonconflictual' (18). The imperial tendencies in this notion of truth are specifically set out by Heidegger in the only opposition that certainty permits, namely the distinction between truth and falsity. False, he notes, is derived from the Latin *falsum* (*falso*) meaning 'fall' (39). To falsify is thus 'to bring to a fall' and with that to command and dominate – returning us to Vattimo's and Zabala's equation of truth with violence, where the politics of dominion is the felling of all opposition by declaring any and every alternative interpretation false.

Heidegger's criticism of this imperial form of politics is also useful as a step towards thinking the conflictual nature of the *demos*. However, to draw this part of the argument to a close it is important to say a few words about Heidegger's treatment of the *polis* (πόλις) in relation to his argument regarding the conflictual essence of truth. First of all, Heidegger points out that, contrary to convention, the *polis* must not be understood as either the city or the state and has no connection to the modern view of the state understood in terms of power. 'The essence of power', he writes, 'is foreign to the πόλις [and] is founded in the metaphysical presupposition that the essence of truth has been transformed into certitude [...]' (91). By contrast, Heidegger proposes, the *polis* must be thought in terms of *alētheia* and the revealing and withdrawal of Being. This he suggests can be seen in the root word *pelein* (πέλειν) meaning 'to be'. The *polis* is thus the place where beings are disclosed and revealed, where Being presences and withdraws, and must therefore be thought as 'the essential abode of man' (90). While no 'modern concept of 'the political' will ever permit anyone to grasp the essence of the πόλις' (91), he writes, because the modern concept of politics is so dominated by the imperium (police) of adequation and certainty, this does not mean that the *polis*, as Heidegger understands it, has no resonance for contemporary politics. If, as Heidegger argues, there is a very strong connection between *polis* and *alētheia*, this means that because *alētheia* 'possesses a conflictual essence [...] then in the πόλις as the essential abode of man there has to hold sway all the most extreme counter-essences' (90). What needs to be shown now is how the *demos* carries with it the counter-essences that come with life in the *polis*.

DEMOS AS HISTORY

In his superb collection *Heretical Essays in the Philosophy of History* Jan Patočka, who studied with Heidegger, and died in custody following police interrogations regarding his involvement with the Czech democratic movement known as Charta 77, takes up the theme of *polemos* in relation to the emergence of both democracy and history. He begins in essay 1 with a definition of freedom as openness (1996:5). This is in line with Heidegger's understanding of freedom as a pre-theoretical openness to the world, to beings, and to the nothing out of which all questioning emerges. Without this openness there is neither creativity nor responsibility. For Patočka, if history signifies anything it is the moment where this openness is made explicit and becomes a philosophical problem. What he calls 'the preproblematic world' is a world of 'pregiven meaning [...]. This world is meaningful [...] because there are therein powers, the demonic, the gods that stand over humans, ruling over them and deciding their destiny' (12). Much in the way the market reigns over everything today, the gods of the preproblematic world took on the police function of regulating everyday life in accordance with a wide range of prescriptions and ordinances aimed at preserving a very specific social order. This is not to say that problematisation was not present, it simply remained concealed or repressed in favour of the 'self-evidence' (13) of life. Likewise, what I have been referring to as 'common sense' can be understood as the persistence of the preproblematic world in its struggle against history. The reason why fundamentalisms and dogmas are so powerful is precisely because of the anxiety induced by the historical realisation that there are no foundations, and that we are radically open to a future of our own making. Fundamentalisms attempt to negate such anxiety by offering a highly prescriptive account of how to think and act. What Patočka calls 'the journey of history' (25) is not simply finding this or that thing to be a problem, but problematising 'the whole as such' (25), and is represented by the emergence of politics and philosophy.

This means that history is not the recording of 'facts', or the 'keeping of annals' (28), but is the 'shaking of life as simply accepted' (41). It is the acceptance of an 'unsheltered life' (38) and the bestowal of a new meaning. While such an unsheltered life is a risk, only by 'confronting it undaunted, can free life as such unfold' (39), and politics be at all possible. This, for Patočka, is definitive of the Western spirit and the beginning of world history, and while he does not include Greek democracy here, but the advent of Greek philosophy, this shaking of sheltered life can only really make sense in relation to the democratic *polis* because only this broke with the naturalness of aristocratic rule which carried with it the unquestioned tradition of the unproblematic world. Only when it is no longer accepted that rule by the best is legitimate, with best being defined by birth and therefore 'nature', can the Greek polis and Greek politics be understood as truly historical.

This is even more the case when Patočka writes: 'The spirit of the *polis* is a spirit of unity in conflict' (41), and then proceeds to offer his own take on the *polemos* that is politics. While he describes *polemos* as the 'power that stands above the opposed parties' (42) he is not suggesting that this is something detached from the conflict and argument that is the lifeblood of politics, rather *polemos* is that which binds opponents together. Just as Heidegger had likened *polemos* to *logos*, to the word or reason that joins people together in their dispute, Patočka states: '*Polemos* is what is common. *Polemos* binds together the contending parties, not only because it stands over them but because in it they are at one' (42). In addition to Vattimo's and Zabbala's hermeneutic communism we have here a polemical communism. One that, in opposition to the sameness of bureaucratic or state communism, still acknowledges the primacy of the common and the collective but understands the nature of that commonality to be open to an interpretive confrontation regarding the world(s) we create. What is most common is our lack of foundation and finality. *Polemos*, for Patočka, is therefore unifying, but the 'unity it founds is more profound than any ephemeral sympathy or coalition of interests: adversaries meet in the shaking of a given meaning and so create a new way of being human – perhaps the only mode that offers hope amid the storm of the world: the unity of the shaken but undaunted' (43).

To avoid any misreading here we cannot take market fundamentalists as an example of the 'shaken but undaunted'. All fundamentalisms would argue that it is important to carry on regardless of any evidence to the contrary, which is precisely the situation we find ourselves in today. We have been shaken, but we are to be undaunted in our commitment to free market messianism. Everywhere we are told to hold our nerve. The socio-economic condition of idiotism has proved itself to be catastrophic and yet the instruction is to continue as before, to not be questioned by the disaster as it unfolds; to deny everything and blame all difficulties on the non-believers. This is the dogmatic inversion of the 'shaken but undaunted', but what Patočka actually asks is for us to have the courage *to be drawn into* the shaking of meaning and invent the world anew: 'This is what history means' (64).

The problem here, of course, remains the politics of commitment. My own concern with proposing an alternative to free market capitalism is that all political change demands commitment to bring a new interpretation into being and such commitment can readily turn into its own dogma that sets itself up in such a way as to guard against any future shaking. This is why the material and physical changes required must be thought in conjunction with a metaphysics that refuses the positivism and realism fundamental to current dogmatisms, be they political, economic or religious. Although this would need working out at length elsewhere, commitment to history as described by Patočka would require something akin to the uncertain fidelity that Alain Badiou (2001:69) describes as a response to the truth that 'punches a "hole" in knowledges [and] is the sole source of new knowledges' (70). Although the Great Financial Crisis was not an event in Badiou's sense of the term – because it was the inevitable outcome of the marriage between third-rate thinking and the unfettered, and therefore blind self-interest of the dominant class – an event can be faintly discerned beneath the 'chat' and that is the mute re-emergence of history.

For Heidegger, fidelity to this re-emergence would not be the faithful recording and transmission of facts, but a fidelity to what he calls 'the inception' (1993). This does not mean we should ignore what we conventionally understand by history because a sense for historicity as the waxing and waning of worlds, especially one that is divorced from teleological visions of progress and completion, is important as a counter to current dogma. Fidelity to the inception, then, is not the search for an immutable and interminable origin that persists throughout time and across all locations in the way that 'nature' or 'God' have been set to work to preserve specific worldviews. For Heidegger, the inception is that moment where the world as a totality of references and assignments, meanings and values emerges as a problem and Dasein comes to understand its essential freedom by positing a new interpretation. In a thinly veiled criticism of Nazism, he writes: 'What is imperishable in the inception does not consist in the longest possible duration of its consequences nor on the furthest possible extension and breadth of its effects, but in the rarity and singularity of each varied return of what is originary within it' (1993:15). As with the concept of the inception, the originary is not a substantial fundament or absolute ground, but an abyss (*Abgrund*), that which punches a hole in knowledge for Badiou; the moment when the nothing becomes manifest. For Heidegger and Patočka that inception is registered for the first time in Greek philosophy – although such a view of beginnings is not without significant problems – and I would like to add in the meeting of the *demos* and the *polis*, or the democratic challenge that interrupted what was previously ordained there.

DEMOCRATIC INCEPTION

To say a little more about the inception or institution of the new and its relation to democracy it is helpful to turn to the work of Cornelius Castoriadis who was also influenced by Heidegger's ontology. For him the politics that is coeval with the emergence of philosophy and democracy 'amounts to the explicit putting into question of the established institution of society' (1991:159). In this reading the polemical nature of the *demos* is the permanent tension between the form (*eidos*) of society already instituted and the instituting imaginary that continually offers innovative images of alternatives. In this regard, what he calls 'democratic philosophy' represented the 'interminable movement' of truth, 'which constantly tests its bounds' and ceased to be the business of priests (160). Again, truth is not to be understood in terms of a correspondence that might be declared adequate and therefore complete, but a response to something that continually happens or takes place as the questioning of what has been instituted. As Heidegger pointed out, once truth is thought in terms of possession, as an adequate correspondence to what we have taken to be reality, 'all remembrance of inception is impossible' (1993:8). Because idiotism takes the market and its related concepts to be in full possession of the truth, any inception, any new ways of thinking and doing can only be viewed as destructive apostasy, warranting both ideological and often physical pre-emptive deterrence.

Ordinarily truth is seen to be the antithesis of history, where universal descriptions are set against particular interpretations, but in the work of Castoriadis the *demos* signifies their coming together as the varied recurrence of a questioning, a challenge and an interruption born of what previously was excluded, hidden or repressed. Democratic politics is therefore the continual creation or '*coming to light*' (Castoriadis 1991:160) of '*another relation*' (160) between the instituting and instituted imagination, and 'does not halt before a conception, given once and for all, of what is just, equal, or free' (Castoriadis 1997:87). Thus, in a manner in keeping with Heidegger and Patočka, Castoriadis argues that the irruption of the *demos* into politics is the 'creation of *historical movement* in the strong sense' (1991:160). History is not the gradual emergence of the true form of human society, but the continual irruption of a polemical truth without end. History is thus the varied return of the inception that takes shape each time a new world is instituted.

While Castoriadis takes the *demos* to be the movement of 'explicit self-institution' (1991:105), by which he means the autonomous modifying of rules under which it lives, such a strong conception of autonomy is problematic because autonomy conventionally privileges the self as the foundation of the law (Curtis 2001). Although in practice idiotism represents every effort to prevent any radical self-reflection, it nevertheless operates through the privileging of the self as a possessive individual and posits the supposedly self-governing individual as the foundation of capitalism's atomistic ethos. Although Castoriadis's vision of autonomy is very far from the individual sovereignty central to idiotism it nevertheless remains a problematic term because the *polemos* of which we are speaking here, as well as the conceptions of truth and inception that accompany it radically undermine the *priority* of the subject and the idea of possession that autonomy usually suggests. To this effect we should note how Castoriadis's own thinking makes advocacy of autonomy in the strong sense already rather difficult.

In his major work *The Imaginary Institution of Society* Castoriadis writes: 'Social imaginary significations place us in the presence of a mode of being which is primary, originary, irreducible' (1987:364). To this mode of being that is the continual disclosure of new forms he gives the name representation or the representative flux, and in this Castoriadis introduces elements of anteriority and alterity that are more in keeping with the heteronomy and ethics of difference found in the work of another pupil of Heidegger's, Emmanuel Levinas: 'The representative flux', writes Castoriadis, 'is, makes itself, as self-alteration, the incessant emergence of the other in and through the positing (*Vor*-stellung) of images or figures' (329). Again, what he calls the instituting imagination is this continual creation of new forms, new visions of social organisation and significance. This conception is even more pronounced when Castoriadis contemplates 'the world' as that which has already been disclosed and instituted. The world is effectively everything we think, say or do, and yet something still 'escapes'. What escapes every instituted world, he writes, 'is the enigma of the world as such, which *stands behind* the common social world, as [...] an inexhaustible supply of otherness, and as an irreducible challenge to every established signification' (371, my italics). Here the various threads of history, truth, and *polemos* are all brought together, and because this is an inherently social creativity – it cannot be otherwise – the work of what he also calls the 'radical imaginary' is always the creation of 'a common world – *kosmos koinos*' (370).

Living and acting in the presence of this mode of being that is irreducible and originary is one way in which the inevitability of closure might be made less constricting and dogmatic. In contrast to Rancière, Castoriadis readily admits that the irruption of the radical imaginary is the 'movement of one closure after another' (1997:105) and yet each form of self-institution emerges out of an enigmatic ground (*Abgrund*) that never permits any claim to adequacy and completion. We give laws to ourselves and posit worlds because these are not given to us already by 'nature' or 'God' acting as the ultimate arkhē – 'the commandment of he who commences' (Rancière 2006:38). The *demos* is thus an interruption in the established order brought about by the continual opening up of questions pertaining to who we are and how we should live together. The *demos* is necessarily polemical and historical representing a challenge to things as they are as well as the temporal shift that registers change. This can only be non-linear history because it cannot be said to be guided by any ultimate goal that would represent the finalisation of an essence, meaning that the notion of a linear history that does have an end and might thereby give rise to a post-historical democracy is a total absurdity. 'Post-historical democracy' is an oxymoron used only by the philosophical equivalent of PR men and marketing executives.

BEYOND THE DOGMA OF IDIOTISM

With the claim that the victory of democracy resulted in the end of history alienation took on a new guise. As was noted in the last chapter alienation in the traditional Marxist conception of the term has been central to the critique of capitalism, but Berardi and others have more recently seen in alienation the possibility of a refusal starting from 'active estrangement' (2009:46). This gap between life and world demands the questioning of labour conditions with the anticipation of potentially revolutionary action to follow. Alienation in the sense that a worker is divorced from the products of their work through the imposition of private property is therefore a prerequisite for change. While alienated labour continues to be a problem in the Western world and is central to concerns over the continued proletarianisation of the global poor, the alienation that emerges under the dogmatic conditions of idiotism separates people from the practice of projecting an alternative future. The narrative of post-historical democracy is designed to disable this essential practice, meaning that a post-historical age is possible only if the *demos* is excised from it. Alienation therefore reigns as the inoculation against any questioning of the current system taken to be the post-historical encapsulation of human endeavour. Given this, it is important we do not permit the closure of post-historical thinking to enter any challenge we posit to idiotism, which is why David Harvey's use of the phrase 'promised land' is so troubling. Such a belief has a long history in Marxism and is best seen in the following quote from the third of Marx's manuscripts of 1844 (Marx, 1970). In the section on 'Private Property and Communism' he extols the wonders of communism as a panacea for every ailment.

> *Communism* as the *positive* transcendence of *private property* as *human self-estrangement,* and therefore as the real *appropriation of the human* essence by and for man; communism therefore as the complete return of man to himself as a *social* (i.e., human) being – a return become conscious, and accomplished within the entire wealth of previous development. This communism, as fully developed naturalism, equals humanism, and as fully developed humanism equals naturalism; it is the *genuine* resolution of the conflict between man and nature and between man and man – the true resolution of the strife between existence and essence, between objectification and self-confirmation, between freedom and necessity, between the individual and the species. Communism is the riddle of history solved, and it knows itself to be this solution. (135)

It is against this kind of messianism that the name *demos* should be assumed. No single interpretation of communism or any other form of politics can be taken as *the* solution, nor should we expect it to take us to the promised land, and yet our being-in-the-world, that is our being-with-others is the only possible place to start. Idiotism is wholly dependent upon the collective and the shared and yet it seeks to disavow it at every turn. As referential totalities our worlds literally make no sense when thought atomistically. From an ecological perspective the idea of bounded, locally closed micro-environments is also nonsensical. Economically the price of commodities involves social dependencies that extend our accountability around the globe. The management of finite resources also requires thinking in terms of a commonality that only the most blinkered dogma can deny. The growing differentiation between rich and poor is ethically unjustifiable given the kinds of mutuality and interconnectivity involved in the processes of globalisation and wealth production, and from the perspective of economics it remains a major fault line within the capitalist system as the world economy becomes dependent on highly unstable trade balances (Raghuram 2010). Idiotism deploys these myriad moments of commonality only to deny them. It atomises in the name of the sovereign individual, and then applies this atomisation to the entire planet. This, is why, as was noted in chapter 1, idiotism is also a globalism (planetarism) and as such it bears all the hallmarks of totalitarianism. This has happened because we have lost sight of the fact that what is most common is our hermeneutic condition, or rather our hermeneutic condition has been reduced to nothing more than the fallaciously conceived expression of individual consumer choices in the post-historical market place of goods and services.

What passes for democracy today is nothing more than a managerial technique for the advancement of oligarchy. This situation must be refused and reclaiming the name *demos* is part of such a refusal. It represents the recovery of the collective (public, social, common) ground that idiotism continues to deploy but continuously denies. Returning to the fact that *demos* deconstructs itself in the sense that it can be understood as both the citizenry and the element that does not yet count, *demos* is both that which preserves the functioning of the state and the given distribution of ways of thinking, speaking and doing, and that which disrupts it or changes who and what counts. In terms of the first function the language of formal democracy certainly plays an absolutely central role in the maintenance of idiotism. Platitudes relating to choice, freedom, and individuality are integral to its syntax and grammar, but even here *demos* can and should register resistance. As was shown in chapter 3, despite its privatisation the money system remains underwritten by the public, and as Mary Mellor has argued, the 'Wall Street socialism' that saved the privatised financial system simply made manifest how 'the notion of private finance is a sham. Privatised money exists by courtesy of the state and the wider public who host it' (2010:162). Here, the meaning of *demos* in the couplet democratic capitalism does not refer to the sovereignty of individuals, but its exact opposite. Capitalism as a system of privatised exchange functions only because it is guaranteed by state authority, but what that actually means is it functions only because it is protected by the state's capacity to raise a levy in the form of taxes from the people. Those who continually promote the importance of privatisation should be reminded that the public and the people – the collective – is what ultimately permits and secures the system of privatised exchange and that as a consequence privatised exchange should only continue if it is of benefit to the entity that ultimately guarantees it. Such an entity is not the individual, or a loose connection of them, but a mutually responsible collective; the *demos*. Without this recognition idiotism remains entirely parasitic on a host it claims does not exist.

Democratic capitalism also, and paradoxically, denies the second meaning of *demos* as that which disrupts the count and challenges the enclosure of the world. *Demos* is at once anarchic and form-giving, emerging out of the nothing from which all questioning arises and yet cannot appear as anything but a projected world, replete with references, assignments and sense. Democratic capitalism is wholly indebted to the social imaginary that refuses any and all closure, and is testimony to a polemical and infinitely creative truth. It is this interpretation of the *demos* as revolutionary movement that gave birth to the modern states that refer to themselves as democratic, but revolution is now deemed illegitimate in our post-historical, even post-millennial times. Of course, as I have already noted, evidence for the existence of the *demos* remains in every uprising and social movement across the planet and is clearly visible in what was been called the Occupy movement and the Arab Spring, although these two specific manifestations of the *demos* when thought in terms of their facticity should not be conflated. The problem here, though, is that such social and political movements can easily revert to party, tribe or nation-based dogmas in which the inception is as swiftly forgotten as it swiftly emerged. These revolutions can also quite easily become the private concerns of those who eventually take power and seize the reins of government, which is why political action needs to rid itself of the metaphysics that continually forgets the polemical character of truth and open itself to the continued presence of alternative interpretations.

As Vattimo and Zabala argue, all theoretical work is thereby charged with the task of intensifying the consciousness of conflict (2011:139). Liberalism (political and economic) sought to mediate such conflict, but because it asserts the autonomous individual as ultimate ground it was completely unable to protect itself against the dogmatic closure it claimed to render impossible. Likewise, pragmatism's attempt to move away from essential and ultimate truths in favour of what 'works' has been unable to divorce itself from a metaphysics of utility, efficiency and quantification. There is much that we can still learn from the liberal and pragmatic traditions, but democratic politics has to fully embrace the lack of ground beyond the activity of human freedom. As Castoriadis noted, all instituting activity institutes a closure, but democratic politics has to understand the provisionality and fallibility of each and every closure, or rather how this provisionality is artificially strengthened through the exercise of power. Against such hierarchical power, politics in the name of the *demos* has to be the pursuit of equality shorn of any predetermined identity, and the advocacy of interpretive confrontation divorced from the belligerence of vested interest.

What is required, then, *is* a revolution, but the *demos* is no war machine of the kind advocated by Tiqqun (2011). It is polemical, but its *polemos* is not reducible to physical conflict. What is necessary is a revolution in our involvement with the world, which does not simply mean a change of guard. In this sense Vattimo's and Zabala's claim that 'armed capitalism is impossible to defeat and [that] a violent acquisition of power would be socially counterproductive' (121) is important to bear in mind. It may be that armed capitalism is actually *not* impossible to defeat in some frontal assault between the people and the military-industrial complex, but even if such a people's army could be amassed the need for violent overthrow begs the question of just how much of the world as it is would need to be broken. Claims that power might submit itself to the people also appeals to some semblance of democratic legitimacy that no longer exists. We live in an age where the people automatically divest themselves of legitimacy once they engage in physical resistance that goes beyond 'peaceful protest'. Secondly, the problem with justifying the level of violence necessary to wipe the slate clean and deliver the promised land also puts us squarely in the camp of other revolutionary movements that declared anything was permitted in their name. As I have already noted a number of times it would be difficult to arouse the requisite commitment and not feel the need to vigorously defend the revolution against all dissent once it has been secured. Against such a war the revolution required is the activation of the *polemos* resistant to all dogma, the one that refuses any ultimate ground or foundation. In this regard Vattimo and Zabala again offer a suitable definition of what such a polemical communism would be: 'Communism's promise of a society "without classes" must be interpreted as "without dominion", that is, […] without an imposed unique truth and compulsory orthodoxy' (116). All of which brings us back to the politics of truth and the role of the university in the recovery of such a polemical principle.

In keeping with the argument regarding managerialism in chapter 4 resistance to idiotism needs to take place in each of those social units that permit idiotism to flood the social field. Of course, the university has always contributed directly to the economy and to industry through a whole range of scientific and technological innovations. It has also been tasked, although implicitly, with contributing to social governance by maintaining a certain hierarchy of knowledge, and with that entrenched class positions, but the university has also been the producer of heterodox thinking and radical knowledge thereby contributing to dramatic social change. However, an important component of idiotism is that research in the natural sciences has increasingly been framed by the need to produce commodifiable end products or technological spin-offs, while research in the human and social sciences is managed in such a way that its genuinely critical potential is lessened, if not totally eradicated through the demand to produce a demonstrable socio-economic 'impact', thereby embedding the logic of 'performativity' (Lyotard 1984) into all academic endeavour. If research does not directly contribute to increased efficiencies in the current socio-economic system or array of power it is regarded as invalid.

Of course, the total incorporation of the university into the ideological practices of idiotism is essential for idiotism's continued dominion. As the only democratic institution to remain in some capacity outside the dogmatic group think it is essential that universities and their staff are brought to heel. As universities increasingly adopt the corporate-consumer model it is becoming more and more difficult for academics to find the time and space to produce the challenging work that is urgently required. Despite the brilliance and undoubted bravery of many journalists the media have increasingly become integral to idiotism's outreach and have seamlessly adopted the confirmatory language of the new common sense to such an extent that it is virtually impossible to find a report that seriously questions the validity of formal democracy or financial capital. There is a sense that a free press may report on whatever it likes so long as it does not challenge the gods of free elections and free enterprise. We are only permitted the pathetic spectacle of the 'humbling' of the Murdochs because rather than showing up the nature of contemporary governance, that is, the operations of oligarchy, it actually supports the absurd idea that oligarchy is still subject to democracy.

Under these conditions the university remains a crucial institution for the support it can give to the various forms of refusal taking place elsewhere. Ironically, however, the only public institution capable of offering a sustained critique of the contemporary formation of capital is now having its funding cut, especially in the UK, because such vast amounts of public money were diverted to bailing out that formation's catastrophic failings. Because the university has always been a public institution that counterposed its role in the structures of governance with its production of heterodox knowledge it has a strong affiliation to the disruption and creativity that is registered in the name *demos* and is the institution that most readily epitomises the interpretive confrontation that is the sign of a polemical conception of truth. This is most pronounced in the field of the humanities which takes as its object of study the being for whom its being is an issue. It is not surprising that in the UK especially the humanities have come under attack for their lack of real world applications. Somehow, it seems to be forgotten that the material of humanities research emerges out of the gap between life and world that raises the question as to who we are and how we should live, and in that it runs counter to the realism so central to idiotism. In an age when it is claimed such questions have been definitively answered humanities research is often presented as an irritant or as anachronistic musing on subjects supposedly 'put to bed' long ago.

This gap out of which renewed questioning will persistently emerge no matter how much human life is enclosed, regulated and managed has its practical analogue in the cracks that John Holloway finds in the uniform surface of contemporary capitalism. He in turn desists from a call for a frontal assault but argues instead that the best defence against the current formation of power is the 'mutual resonance of ordinary rebelliousness' (2010:258). His call is to 'open the enclosed' by using the existing cracks to doing things differently: 'Make holes [...]. Create cracks and let them expand [...], let them flow together' (261). Wherever there is an exchange between people that is neither commodified nor resulting in the production of surplus value there is a crack in the uniformity of capitalist exchange relations. Likewise, wherever there is the mute stirring of the intuition that all is not well with the world, so the polemical truth essential to the *demos* is also manifest, and the university has an important role to play in helping such questioning flourish. This does not mean it must invest in producing and disseminating a new kind of knowledge, but that it must help create spaces where the world becomes a problem. These are therefore not simply spaces for furthering knowledge, but places for the contestation of our being-in-the-world.

In something of a throwaway line Holloway remarks that he is happy to be one of the 'fools who live in the cracks' (253), but the fool must play a greater role. Against the idiot that encapsulates contemporary power we must demand the full return of the fool. Before the fool was reduced to the madman – pathologised, medicalised and incarcerated – the fool sat at the sovereign's side, a reminder of human hubris and the dangers of becoming enthralled by one's own power. There is a tendency now to think of the fool in relation to the jester and to courtly entertainment and spectacle, but the fool primarily marked the limitations of knowledge and the fact that a world might at any point be turned upside down. The fool thereby epitomised the polemical truth that the world is built over an abyss. The fool also had strong cultural ties to itinerancy and homelessness, representing the journeying that is integral to all human endeavour, and was central to collective celebrations that mocked authority (Bakhtin 1984). Now that we have supposedly arrived, and are building a permanent and universally applicable home in the shadows of the market, the fool has been dispensed with and idiots are everywhere resplendent, satisfied that there is nothing to know beyond the laws of supply and demand. The only advantage is that idiotism is so near-sighted that it cannot see how the dispensed with fool has not gone away but has merely been set free to wander and explore the cracks. Research in the humanities must therefore follow the fool into these cracks and open up every fissure and fracture that appear in the representations of the world and the discursive practices that manage it. Teaching, too, must follow the path of the fool. As Bill Readings wrote in his study *The University in Ruins*, marking out the difference between epistemology and ontology, we should not be looking to re-centre ourselves and our students around an alternative political programme that may in the end turn out to be as dogmatic as idiotism, we should be *decentring* ourselves (Readings 1997:153). In an especially Lyotardian register he argues that we should heighten our sense of dissensus, heterogeneity and difference, that we should focus on the obligations and responsibilities arising from the pursuit of justice rather than the declarations made in the name of truth, but it might equally be said that we need to decentre both our research and teaching around the polemical truth that takes the name *demos*.

Bibliography

Ahamed, Liaquat (2010) *Lords of Finance*, London: William Heinemann.

Akerlof, George A. and Robert J. Shiller (2009) *Animal Spirits: How Human Psychology Drives the Economy, and Why it Matters for Global Capitalism*, Princeton: Princeton University Press.

Althusser, Louis (1984) 'Ideology and Ideological State Apparatuses', *Essays on Ideology*, London, Verso.

Althusser, Louis (2003) *The Humanist Controversy and Other Writings*, François Metheron (ed.), London: Verso.

Aristotle (1998) *The Metaphysics*, London: Penguin.

Aristotle (1987) *De Anima (On the Soul)*, London: Penguin.

Badiou, Alain (2001) *Ethics: An Essay on the Understanding of Evil*, London: Verso.

Bakhtin, Mikhael (1984) *Rabelais and his World*, Bloomington: Indiana University Press.

Barthes, Roland (1973) *Mythologies*, London: Paladin Books.

Bataille, George (1989) *Theory of Religion*, New York: Zone Books.

Beck, Ulrich (1999) *What is Globalization?* Cambridge: Polity Press.

Bellamy, John and Fred Magdoff (2009) *The Great Financial Crisis*, New York: Monthly Review Press.

Berardi, Franco (2009) *The Soul at Work: From Alienation to Autonomy*, New York: Semiotext(e).

Bull, Michael (2000) *Sounding Out the City*. Oxford: Berg.

Carey, James (1989) *Communication as Culture*, Boston: Unwin Hyman.

Castoriadis, Cornelius (1987) *The Imaginary Institution of Society*, Cambridge: Polity Press.

Castoriadis, Cornelius (1991) *Philosophy, Politics, Autonomy: Essays in Political Philosophy*, New York: Oxford University Press.

Castoriadis, Cornelius (1997) *World in Fragments: Writings on Politics, Society, Psychoanalysis, and the Imagination*, Stanford: Stanford University Press.

Cohen, Stanley and Laurie Taylor (1992) *Escape Attempts: The Theory and Practice of Resistance in Everyday Life*. London: Routledge.

Cooper, Melinda (2008) *Life as Surplus: Biotechnology and Capitalism in the Neoliberal Era*, Seattle: University of Washington Press.

Critchley, Simon (2007) *Infinitely Demanding: Ethics of Commitment, Politics of Resistance*, London: Verso.

Curtis, Neal (2001) *Against Autonomy: Lyotard, Judgement and Action*, Aldershot: Ashgate Publishing.

Curtis, Neal (2006) *War and Social Theory: World, Value, Identity*, Basingstoke: Palgrave.

Dean, Jodi (2002) *Publicity's Secret: How Technoculture Capitalizes on Democracy*, Ithaca: Cornell University Press.

Dean, Jodi (2009) *Democracy and Other Neoliberal Fantasies: Communicative Capitalism and Left Politics*, Durham NC: Duke University Press.

DeLander, Manuel (1991) *War in the Age of Intelligent Machines*. New York: Zone Books.

Deleuze, Gilles (1992) 'Postscript to the Societies of Control' *October*, vol. *59*. Winter, 1992.

DeMartino, George (2000) *Global Economy, Global Justice: Theoretical and Policy Alternatives to Neoliberalism*. London: Routledge.

Enteman, Willard F. (1993) *Managerialism: The Emergence of a New Ideology*, Madison: University of Wisconsin Press.

Fried, Gregory (2000) *Heidegger's Polemos: From Being to Politics*, New Haven: Yale University Press.

Friedman, Milton (1966) *Essays in Positive Economics*, Chicago: University of Chicago Press.

Friedman, Milton and Anna Jacobson Schwartz (1971) *A Monetary History of the United States, 1867-1960*. Princeton, NJ: Princeton University Press.

Friedman, Milton (2002) *Capitalism and Freedom*, Chicago: University of Chicago Press.

Fukuyama, Francis (1992) *The End of History and the Last Man*, London: Penguin Books.

Galbraith, John Kenneth (2009) *The Economics of Innocent Fraud*, London: Penguin Books.

Gramsci, Antonio (1971) *Selections from the Prison Notebooks*, London: Lawrence and Wishart.

Greenspan, Alan (1967) 'Antitrust' in Ayn Rand, *Capitalism: The Unknown Ideal*, New York: Signet.

Habermas, Jürgen (1992) *The Structural Transformation of the Public Sphere*, Cambridge: Polity Press.

Hardt, Michael and Antonio Negri (2000) *Multitude*, Cambridge, MA: Harvard University Press.

Harvey, D. (1999) *The Limits of Capital*, London: Verso Books.

Harvey, D. (2003) *The New Imperialism*, Oxford: Oxford University Press.

Harvey, D. (2005) *A Brief History of Neoliberalism*, Oxford: Oxford University Press.

Harvey, D. (2010) *The Enigma of Capital*, London: Profile Books.

Hayek, F.A. (2007) *The Road to Serfdom*, Chicago: University of Chicago Press.

Heidegger, Martin (1962) *Being and Time*, Oxford: Basil Blackwell.

Heidegger, Martin (1993) *Basic Concepts*, Bloomington: Indiana University Press.

Heidegger, Martin (1995) *The Fundamental Concepts of Metaphysics*, Bloomington: Indiana University Press.

Heidegger, Martin (1996) *Being and Time*, New York: SUNY Press.

Heidegger, Martin (1996) *Hölderlin's Hymn 'The Ister'*, Bloomington: Indiana University Press.

Heidegger, Martin (1998) *Pathmarks*, Cambridge: Cambridge University Press.

Heidegger, Martin (1999) *Ontology—The Hermeneutics of Facticity*, Bloomington: Indiana University Press.

Heidegger, Martin (2001) *Phenomenological Interpretations of Aristotle*, Bloomington: Indiana University Press.

Heidegger, Martin (2002) *Off The Beaten Track*, Cambridge: Cambridge University Press.

Hirst, Paul (2001) *War and Power in the 21st Century*, Cambridge: Polity Press.

Holloway, John (2010) *Crack Capitalism*, London: Pluto Press.

Hosking, Geoffrey (2010) *Trust: Money, Markets and Society*, London: Seagull Books.

Johnson, Simon and James Kwak (2010) *13 Bankers: The Wall Street Takeover and the Next Financial Meltdown*, New York: Pantheon Books.

Joxe, Alain (2002) *Empire of Disorder*. New York: Semiotext(e).

Kagan, Robert (2008) *The Return of History and the End of Dreams*, New York: Alfred A. Knopf.

Klein, Naomi (2007) *The Shock Doctrine: The Rise of Disaster Capitalism*, London: Penguin.

Krugman, Paul (2008) *The Return of Depression Economics and the Crisis of 2008*, New York: Allen Lane.

Lanchester, J. (2010) *Whoops! Why Everyone Owes Everyone and No One Can Pay*, London: Penguin Books.

Lee, Martyn J. (1993) *Consumer Culture Reborn: The Cultural Politics of Consumption*, London: Routledge.

Leiss, William, et al (2005) *Social Consumption in Advertising: Consumption in the Mediated Marketplace*, London: Routledge.

Liu, Lydia (2011) *The Freudian Robot: Digital Media and the Future of the Unconscious*, Chicago: University of Chicago Press.

Locke, John (1952) *The Second Treatise of Government*, Indianapolis: Bobbs-Merrill.

Lyotard, Jean-François (1984) *The Postmodern Condition: A Report on Knowledge*, Manchester: University of Manchester Press.

Marazzi, Christian (2008) *Capital and Language: From the New Economy to the War Economy*, New York: Semiotext(e).

Marazzi, Christian (2010) *The Violence of Financial Capital*, New York: Semiotext(e).

Marx, Karl (1970) *Economic and Philosophic Manuscripts of 1844*, London: Lawrence and Wishart Ltd.

McDonagh, Patrick (2008) *Idiocy: A Cultural History*, Liverpool: Liverpool University Press.

McGuigan, Jim (2009) *Cool Capitalism*, London: Pluto Press.

McMurtry, John (2002) *Value Wars: The Global Market Versus the Life Economy*, London: Pluto Press.

Mellor, Mary (2010) *The Future of Money*, London: Pluto Press.

Miller, Daniel (2001) 'The Poverty of Morality', *Journal of Consumer Culture*, vol. 1, no. 2, July 2001.

Mouffe, Chantal (1993) *The Return of the Political*, London: Verso.

Newman, F.W. (1856) *The Iliad of Homer*, London: Walton and Maberly.

Nietzsche, Friedrich (1968) *The Will to Power*, New York: Vintage Books.

Nietzsche, Friedrich (1989) *Beyond Good and Evil: Prelude to a Philosophy of the Future*, New York: Vintage Books.

Pariser, Eli (2011) *The Filter Bubble: What the Internet is Hiding from You*, London: Penguin/Viking.

Patočka, Jan (1996) *Heretical Essays in the Philosophy of History*, Chicago: Open Court.

Polt, Richard (2007) 'Beyond Struggle and Power: Heidegger's Secret Resistance', *Interpretation*, vol. 35, no. 1, Fall 2007, 11-40.

Potts, Tracey (2010) 'Mobile Technology and the Everyday', unpublished research paper, Centre for Critical Theory, University of Nottingham.

Quiggin, John (2010) *Zombie Economics: How Dead Ideas Still Walk Among Us*, Princeton: Princeton University Press.

Raghuram, Rajan, G. (2010) *Fault Lines: How Hidden Fractures Still Threaten the World Economy*, Princeton, NJ: Princeton University Press.

Rancière, Jacques (1999) *Disagreement: Politics and Philosophy*, Minneapolis: University of Minnesota Press.

Rancière, Jacques (2006) *The Hatred of Democracy*, London: Verso.

Rand, Ayn (1964) *The Virtue of Selfishness*, New York: Signet.

Rand, Ayn (1967) *Capitalism: The Unknown Ideal*, New York: Signet.

Readings, Bill (1997) *The University in Ruins*, Cambridge, MA: Harvard University Press.

Robinson, T.M. (1987) *Heraclitus: Fragments*, Toronto: University of Toronto Press.

Robinson, William I. (2004) *A Theory of Global Capitalism: Production, Class, and State in a Transnational World*, Baltimore: The Johns Hopkins University Press.

Scahill, Jeremy (2007) *Blackwater: The Rise of the World's most Powerful Mercenary Army*, New York: Serpent's Tail.

Schattschneider, Elmer E. (1960) *The Semi-Sovereign People: A Realist's View of Democracy in America*, New York: Holt, Reinhart and Winston.

Schramm, Wilbur (1971) 'The Nature of Communication Between Humans', *The Process and Effects of Mass Communication*, revised edition, edited by Wilbur Schramm and Donald F. Roberts, Urbana: University of Illinois Press.

Sennett, Richard (2002) *The Fall of Public Man*, London: Penguin Books.

Sennett, Richard (2006) *The Culture of the New Capitalism*, New Haven: Yale University Press.

Shiva, Vandana (2000) *Stolen Harvest: The Hijacking of the Global Food Supply*, London: Zed Books.

Shiva, Vandana (2003) 'Food Rights, Free Trade and Fascism', *Globalizing Rights*, Matthew J. Gibney (ed.), Oxford: Oxford University Press.

Sinclair, Timothy J. (2005) *The New Masters of Capital: American Bond Rating Agencies and the Politics of Creditworthiness*, Ithaca: Cornell University Press.

Sklair, Leslie (2000) *The Transnational Capitalist Class*, Oxford: Blackwell Publishers.

Slater, Don (1997) *Consumer Culture and Modernity*, Cambridge: Polity Press.

Smith, Adam (1998) *Wealth of Nations*, Oxford: Oxford University Press.

Social Finance (2009) 'Social Impact Bonds: Rethinking Finance for Social Outcomes', Social Finance, August, 2009. www.socialfinance.org.uk/resources/socialfinance/social-impact-bonds

Southwood, Ivor (2011) *Non-Stop Inertia*, Winchester: Zero Books.

Stirner, Max (1993) *The Ego and Its Own*, London: Rebel Press.

Tiqqun (2011) *This is Not a Program*, New York: Semiotext(e).

Turkle, Sherry (1995) *Life on the Screen: Identity in the Age of the Internet*, London: Phoenix.

Turkle, Sherry (2011) *Alone Together: Why we Expect More from Technology and Less from Each Other*, New York: Basic Books.

Vattimo, Gianni, and Santiago Zabala (2011) *Hermeneutic Communism: From Heidegger to Marx*, New York: Columbia University Press.

Williams, Raymond (1965) *The Long Revolution*, London: Pelican Books.

Williams, Raymond (1974) *Television: Technology and Cultural Form*, London: Fontana.

Žižek, Slavoj (2005) *Interrogating the Real*, London: Continuum.

Index

Milton Keynes UK
Ingram Content Group UK Ltd.
UKHW011605201123
432923UK00003B/117